What people are saying abc　　　　　　　　　:

Whispers of the Morning, is a book written for the WOMAN. The Woman that works hard every day to keep her body, soul, and spirit in shape. The woman that is broken yet strong. The woman that has it all together and the one that is struggling to keep it all together. Whatever description fits the woman you are, this book takes you on an extraordinary journey of grace through life's billows. A journey that emphasises God's infinite and immense love for you in a very real and relatable way.

From a collection of personal experiences she calls the 'Muse', to the 'Pause' reflection on God's dealings and the 'Parables', expressions of true beauty within, Mrs. Macaulay, in this book, relays the essence of understanding that God's presence is not something we go after, pick up and then drop it to pick it again later. God's presence is in us, with us and for us. And no matter what we go through, even in our silent whispers, God is there and His grace is sufficient.

—Dr. Samuel Ekundayo
Author, Academic, Preacher,
Life Coach and Motivational Speaker.
Auckland, New Zealand.

Whispers of the Morning' is what I call that early morning book that is best read when you can take the time to read and ruminate over the lessons shared. Encouraging, inspiring and thought provoking, it has been a somewhat profound and emotional read for me.

Sola takes you on an introspective soul searching journey using her personal experiences and walk with God, to provoke you to think just a little bit deeper, beyond what appears, to what actually is. In her simple, candid and engaging way this read is a therapeutic journey that ultimately draws you to the heart of God.

Olufunmi Olajoyegbe
Singer, Songwriter, Trustee - GiG Time Reforms Foundation
Lagos, Nigeria

Whispers of the Morning tripped me into a paradigm shift to see into the light of the Divine Norm.

There is an abnormality of usual prevalence in Christendom today and these are perspectives from human presumptions that contradict God's divine thoughts, ways and words.

The 'Abnormality of Usual' enlightens my mind on the Divine Norm. This I see through as the inspiration for the book; a departure from the usual Christian book. This book is indeed an abnormality of the Usual.

I go with these paradigm shifts from the usual norms.

Do I truly need to SHOUT to be heard by God? The chapter got me into a musing mood. Did Elijah have a shouting contest with the prophets of Baal on mount Carmel, before he called to God to prove Himself? Did God speak to Elijah in the cleft of the rock amidst the wind, fire and earthquake? Elijah called to God effortlessly in simple faith without physical exertion and fire came down from heaven. And the LORD spoke in a still quiet voice.

The church seems to have devised its own weapons of warfare and methods for the great commission. Mostly 'Abnormality of the Usual' but the chapter

'Be Beautiful, Seven Different Ways' tripped me into the DIVINE NORM Ephesians 6:13-18.

The book takes us back to the ancient landmarks outlined in the scriptures, of which the LORD admonishes His children not to shift.

In a nutshell 'Whispers of the Morning' is an inspiration of the Divine Norm so timely for this dispensation.

An easy to read book that retains its cogent thoughts.

Well done, Sola.

Arinola Oniyide
Educator, Sunday school Teacher
An avid reader.
Lagos, Nigeria

Whispers of the Morning

an inspirational journal

SOLA MACAULAY

Whisper of the Morning

Copyright © 2017 by Sola Macaulay

Unless otherwise noted, all Scripture is taken from the King James Version of the Bible. Scripture quotations marked NKJV are taken from the New King James Version®. Copyright © 1982 by Thomas Nelson, Inc., Used by permission. All rights reserved; MSG are taken from *THE MESSAGE*. Copyright © by Eugene H. Peterson 1993, 2002. Used by permission.

Copyright © 1954, 1987 by The Lockman Foundation. Used by permission. (www. Lockman.org.); NIV are taken from the Holy Bible, New International Version®, NIV®. Copyright © 1973, 2011 by Biblica, Inc.TM Used by per- mission of Zondervan. All rights reserved worldwide. www.zondervan.com.

Paperback: ISBN 978-978-964--043-0

Hardcover: ISBN 978-978-964-044-7

Jedidiah Publications Limited

jedidiahpubltd@gmail.com

+234-7080317274

Cover design by Damonza

Interior design by Damonza

Dedication:

To all my sisters everywhere who love God tenaciously and drive sound Bible knowledge as their watchword, thank you for teaching 'the word', regardless. You've got Heaven's backing. You are courageous women of a mighty God.

Preface

My voice shalt thou hear in the morning, O Lord; in the morning will I direct my prayer unto thee, and will look up. Psalm 5:3 (KJV)

When life alters your normalcy,
For a moment you grasp the pain
That it temporarily brings.
What you may fail to see
Is the tide that moves away from
Pain to new sightings of life.
Through tear streaked eyes
You ought to see the waterfall
That splashes against the rocks,
Like unchanging hope
That births new springs of life.
So when next life alters your normalcy,
Grasp the pain, for behind the peel
Is a fresh new life
That it brings with it.

LET ME COMMEND to you my second book, ***Whispers of the Morning.***

At the time I was preparing to publish my first book, ***Petals of Grace***, the Lord laid it in my heart to work on this book next. Excitedly, I got started, and then got stuck. I had issues of life to deal with.

I started writing **Whispers of the Morning** during a somewhat turbulent time in my life. Turbulence seemed rife in the lives of those around me as well. Often, it would seem the troubles were so rooted there could be no way out. I re-read **Petals of Grace** and I thought of how bright and flowery it was compared with some parts of this book, which would capture the darker times. It would seem also that the groans of my morning, the whispers in God's ears, were meant to be the fodder for most of what you will read in this book.

Who knew I would go through a tunnel where it seemed I might not be able to see the light of dawn? I was asked the question, Where is your God? We as followers and servants must bear our crosses. This book will never give any undue attention to the works of darkness. Rather it will showcase God's triumph over the works of darkness. Instead I will glory in my infirmities like my brother, Apostle Paul. I am grateful for the many woes, pain, oppositions and adversities that I had to endure. It has placed and continues to place me in the path of refinement and fulfilment of my purpose. No pain will ever be wasted. When we choose to suffer for Christ, greatness is assured.

What will you read in this book? Series of observations and events of life lived by the grace of God. There are three sections: The Muse Section, where I dig inside of me. What's going on is the question I asked; The Pause Section, where I got 'sent off to bed for being naughty' by God, and then the Picture Section, where I tried to stoke the imagination and paint a picture with words. All these are interwoven with the theme of grace again and again and reiterate that fact that God loves us infinitely, even though there will be times when we face unimaginable pain. Yet in life, we win. God's plans for our lives are grand such that that no matter what we face we'll be able to come out on top and we will always win. Do remember that God's version of success is very different from ours. Don't ever use man's version to determine the course of your life and rule yourself out when you think you don't make the cut or meet the standard.

Let me encourage you in this: In this life we will have tribulation, but be of good cheer for I have overcome the world. Those are Jesus' words of assurance and my reminder too. You can whisper in God's ears. All you have to do is whisper and He can hear you.

One day I left the house in a hurry because I needed to get somewhere and I was already late. I didn't have my usual 'quiet time' where I would take my time over a languorous study of the Bible, stay still over one verse of scripture and write notes upon notes before moving on to the next verse. When I got into the car, I remembered I hadn't prayed. I hadn't said a word to the Lord and I was going to face the day. I became downcast. Just as I thought about redeeming the time, the Holy Spirit whispered to me, 'I'm as close as your next breath. You can talk with me anytime. The same God who created the ears and the whispers can hear our whispers. A whisper would have been enough.' God can read our thoughts as well as understand perfectly our 'whispers of the morning.' The whispers of pain, of joy, of praise, any whispers at all; God catches them even before our next breath.

Have you whispered to God today?

Blessings,
Sola Macaulay
Lagos, Nigeria
December 2017

Acknowledgements

In writing this book, whilst I was travelling through a somewhat dark tunnel, I experienced the awesomeness and greatness of God in an unprecedented way. Like the children of Israel, I saw God fight for me. I saw God lift up His banner of love over me. That banner of love was tangible through the unusual strength I found myself displaying in the face of adversity. When the Lord assures me time and time again that He loves me, I would often feel like I'm being borne on eagle's wings. He comforted me like a loving Father would. I am eternally grateful to God my father.

Dear Holy Spirit, thank You for the inspiration to write, the light that shines in the dark places, the available resources and help from every quarter. That inspiration that sparks in my heart is all because of You.

Sweet Jesus, thank You for loving me endlessly. In my own little way, You made me walk on water. I love You because You love me. I love You because You are love. I love You because I just love You. I cannot find the words...

To my Bible gist partners: Thank you for the times of refreshing; rightly dividing the undiluted word of God. I love those bible chats. Those times of fellowship are what have kept me believing I am truly surrounded by covenant friends. Thank you for always responding to my phone calls. Your chats have been inspiring, encouraging, and have helped keep me steady in times of discouragement.

To my husband and daughter, you encourage every step I take as I obey the Lord. You patiently endure those moments when I'm locked into a zone trying to find the light out of the tunnel so I can put down eloquently what I have been inspired and instructed to write. I love you with all of me.

To my parents, thank you for a wonderful childhood filled with good memories.

To my sisters and brother, I couldn't have asked for better siblings. Love you always.

To my editor, Joy Ehonwa, I have enjoyed every moment working with you. You are detailed and thorough. Thank you.

Foreword

"I didn't do anything wrong". My phone fell limply to my side. 'I did not do anything wrong". I said these words over and over under my breath, blinking back the hot tears. How did Sola Macaulay know about this burdensome thought I had been carrying around since Sholly, my sister passed on. How did she know that I felt that I had done something that left my sister open and vulnerable? I had never shared this with anyone. A wave of relief washed over me as I picked up my phone and continued reading "What did I do wrong?"

That was to be the first of many times God would speak to me, hug me, teach me, assure me, wipe away my tears, and steady me using his daughter, Sola Macaulay as His Oracle. When people ask me to write their forewords, I regard it a huge honour and privilege. A book is such a personal thing so being considered for this role is special and I don't take it lightly. But this time, I felt it was something more and I was right.

I was given the assignment to do this foreword more for my sake than anything else. There was something in this book that God wanted me to get. Dear Reader, I got what God had for me. My mind was dealing with so much and many times I really did not know how to process them. To voice them out would have been quite disheartening to those I held dear. God knew. So, he sent me this assignment as part of my healing process.

I don't know what you are dealing with but your assignment today is to read this book with the ears of your heart. That you hold this book in your hand is no happenstance. God sees your heart too and knows you have questions. I promise you. You will find answers in this book. They may be tucked away in the main text or maybe even in the introductory verses or the closing action gems. If you read expectant, you will find them.

But you must be still and you must be ready to experience many mind-set shifts. Many things you thought you knew about walking with God may just be about to change. Most importantly, dear Reader, you must be prepared to find a quiet place where you can mute all the noise around you. Because God is about to speak to you and most likely, his messages will come as ***Whispers of the Morning***.

Bola (Salt) Essien-Nelson
Author, Speaker, Coach, Editor
www.saltchronicles.com

Contents

THE MUSE

In the multitude of my *thoughts* within me thy
comforts delight my soul. Psalm 94:19

1. Bring Me a Minstrel

Bring me a minstrel,
Let him sing
Songs about my Saviour
Happily.
Words of adoration
Please Him,
Beat the drums and gong
Let me dance
Gleefully and cheerfully
In my Saviour's arms.

I heard God whisper to me, 'Bring me a minstrel.'

'But now bring me a minstrel. And it came to pass, when the minstrel played, that the hand of the Lord came upon him.' (2 Kings 3:15, King James Version)

I love music. I see people who don't care very much for music as living less than full lives. I love to dance although I can only wiggle these days. Gone are the days of nimble fluid movements. Sad to say, but old age catches up every now and then.

The thing about music is that it is more than just the sound we hear. There's a concrete message inbuilt in it. There's an atmosphere, a spirit, a world created when we sing or listen to music. Music is much more powerful than we think.

Way back, before I knew the Lord, I purchased a 'ghetto blaster' cassette player from the vacation money my dad gave me. I was proud of my new set and had gone to a friend's house to get him to 'dub' loads of music in different genres: Jazz, soul, blues…name it. For me, your taste in music was a class thing. Mature minds like jazz, etc. I had as many as a hundred cassettes. I was on top of the world. Music to help me study, music to help me sleep, music to get over trauma and many more therapeutic uses. I needed music like water.

Shortly after settling down with my new toy, I received Christ into my heart. My love for music didn't change, but herein lay the problem: I couldn't listen to the old music anymore. I knew instinctively that something was wrong with it. I had a hundred cassettes of 'uninspiring' music as far as my newfound faith was concerned. I had invested so much time and energy getting it all together; it took my friend and me two days of continuous recording to get such a varied collection.

This was the first test of my loyalty to my newfound faith. To listen or not? Or better still, to trash or not? I recognized that music did something to/for me. The combo of melody and words created an atmosphere that was so real it changed what I felt inside. Music always fixed me up.

So what's the big deal? What's changed? Why can't I listen to the same music? After all it is just music isn't it? Before I answer that question, let's take a peek at the contextual story of our text above.

King Jehoram, king of Israel, was facing a battle against the king of Moab and he had enlisted the help of King Jehoshaphat, king of Judah. They met a stumbling block on the way when the wilderness they passed through produced no water and they feared for their lives and the lives of their host and cattle. At that point, they strongly believed they were out of God's will. However, Jehoshaphat, who was still very much in touch with God, suggested they send for the prophet Elisha to know God's will. Elisha then sent for a minstrel; the equivalent of a worship minister.

In an atmosphere of worship, God stepped into the situation and they won the battle. Jehoshaphat knew they desperately needed God. The worship music more or less invoked the presence of God. God inhabits the praises/worship of His people. We are assured of this: *'But thou art Holy, Oh thou that inhabitest the praises of Israel.' (Psalm 22:3, KJV)*

God loves our praise and worship and is attracted to a life of praise. God should be our object of praise/worship.

The devil used to be the worship leader in Heaven before he messed up. His plan has always been and still is to steal the focus of praise/worship from God to himself. He inspires the variety of music today that sound so nice and almost so heavenly, yet is directed at hell. They come in soul stirring melodies to inspire the mind to make oneself or a lover the object of our adoration. They come in seductive melodies to invoke a corresponding physical yearning for sordid affairs, crazy moments, and all manner of wild party modes. The enemy gets his kicks from diverting our adoration from God. He knows there's no middle ground. Once you're not on God's side, you're definitely on his side.

Look at another example. Evil spirits often tormented King Saul, and one of his subjects suggested inviting a minstrel to play soothing music. They sent for David, the worshipper. Undoubtedly, David played worship music because the object of his songs was God. Every time David played his harp, the evil spirits left King Saul. There's something powerful about music and the kind of atmosphere it creates that most people are clueless about.

If you're a born-again child of the Most High God, you definitely need to pay attention to the kind of music you listen to. When the music plays, who do you think is hovering around your atmosphere; God's awesome presence or some demonic infestations?

When you bring in the minstrel, make sure that his worship voice, instrument and melody all point towards Heaven.

Ponder this:

Was music a thing for you before you met Christ? Have you found yourself sometimes lapsing into the soulful music of the past? Have you keyed into worship music? Please do. You'll never find the basis for comparison.

2. What Did I Do Wrong?

Some pain in life
Often lingers on.
Bereft of comfort
We start to question.
Yet often it's not wrong
That we do when we stand,
It's the pain of standing
That seems so wrong.
Yet be assured
That though pain lingers,
Rejoicing is longer;
It's forever.

The children of Israel were in captivity yet were in God's will. God orchestrated the entire sojourn in Egypt. (See Exodus 3:1-10).

A close friend had been through hell and high water and I became a little encumbered by thoughts of why. I wondered if she deserved all she'd been going through. I was inclined to believe it wasn't fair. On the other hand, I knew that all things worked together for good, to those that love God and are called according to His purpose (Romans 8:28). That's what the word of God declares: simple and pretty straightforward. I mused and paced back and forth and then decided to just let the case rest. It was clearly in God's hands and there really was nothing I could do about it.

During my devotion, I was flipping through the book of Exodus, not decidedly doing an intense study or anything of the sort. I'd merely glanced at the well-known story of Moses and the burning bush when the Lord dropped this question in my spirit, 'What did the children of Israel do wrong that caused them to be enslaved for four hundred and thirty years?'

Now let's see...Joseph's brothers sold him to Egypt. Only Egypt was big enough to contain the dream God gave him about his future. Even though it started out like a pathetic case, God could've rescued Joseph from his scheming brothers but He didn't. Obviously, Joseph was already on track. The ball had already been set in motion. Nothing wrong in there! He didn't go to Egypt because he wanted to. He didn't even know he would end up in Egypt or that Egypt would be his Rehoboth. He didn't do anything wrong.

Finally, after all the twists and turns, Joseph becomes the second most powerful man in the entire Egyptian region. He didn't do anything wrong there, did he? In fact, he did everything right, like refusing the advances of a married woman, with 'wrong' consequences. Then comes the famine, the moment of reckoning: The real reason why God catapulted Joseph to Egypt. Papa Jacob (Israel) and his entire household moved to Egypt, to escape famine and to be with Joseph, his favourite child. What did he do wrong? Nothing! Wouldn't you do the same if you were Israel? Wouldn't you be happy to see your long lost child and die in his arms? Wouldn't you be happy to find out that you don't have to watch each of your children and their children die of famine? Great! I thought so too.

They did nothing wrong, yet after flourishing in Egypt for so long, a new king ascends the throne. It's as though he was carefully programmed not to have any record of the existence of Joseph and his descendants. What? Not even a record in the history books? And then the children of Israel were plunged into the darkness of slavery for so many years. What did they do wrong to this particular king and his generations thereafter apart from them being intimidated by the sheer population of the children of Israel? Nothing!

Israel languished in anguish and pain with no hope of deliverance. The children born during this era lived and died without knowing any other existence but slavery. What did they do wrong?

Absolutely nothing!

Then one day, God threw a burning bush in the mix and the plan of deliverance started a chain of events. The children of Israel were going to be freed. What did they do right? Nothing! It all had to do with God's purpose and timing.

I pondered over these events and got really excited. I grabbed my phone and punched in the numbers of two of my Bible chat friends and we discussed. I could see clearly and I hope you do too.

Sometimes even when we're right in the centre of the will of God, we face adversity. No, you didn't do anything wrong. God has a plan, a purpose. Not yet convinced? Okay, look at the story of the man born blind in John 9:1-12. They asked Jesus the pertinent question, who sinned? Why was the man born blind? Surely, someone must have messed up generations before. Jesus erased their erroneous thinking by saying neither the man's father nor mother had sinned. It all had to do with God's plan and purpose, and His glory.

Sometimes we do the guilt trip thing and assume every time we get an 'ouch' out of life, it must mean God is mad at us. No, it doesn't always work like that. If it did, we'd all be in soup daily. God allows us to go through adversity for so many reasons. Sometimes it is to help build our character. Sometimes, God doesn't make it obvious nor does He give us a reason. We just have to trust that because His love for us is infinite, He always has our best interest at heart. These seeming concentric circles of pain are not meant to destroy or kill us or make life unbearable. They're meant for a far worthier weight of glory.

I'm sorry if you're going through sizzling hot oil right now, or dealing with an impossible situation. If it's not an obvious fault of yours then please hang in there. You didn't do anything wrong, Honey. God is working it all out for your own good. Just hang in there. You're almost at the finish line.

Ponder this:

Have you ever felt like everything you do is wrong? That maybe God is angry with you? Listen; though God allows us to go through things for a divine purpose, His love for you is intact and unconditional. Bask in it and never feel condemned.

3. The Absurdity of the Normal

When God speaks,
His truths He reveals.
What seems so contrary
To every man's norm,
Are God's ways of saying,
I am God after all.

A friend and I were chatting the other day. This was just a few hours after she lost her brother. We talked about understanding God's sovereign will. We talked about people expecting things in their lives to follow a certain pattern. Grow up, finish school, get married, bucket load of kids, good business or job and then retirement. That's what people expect and want in life. That's what people term normal. My friend asked the question, who defines normal? That made me pause. I took in a deep, strong breath and exhaled loudly.

That is a million dollar question. Who defines normal? What's normal about being born into slavery? What's normal about never having children, getting married in your 50s or never marrying at all?

I found a new definition of normal. Normal isn't when everyone is in tune and doing the same thing whether wrong or not. Normal is not when everyone becomes unaffected by your life. Normal is when what you say shocks people who are under the influence of the prince of the power of the air. Normal is when your life flows upstream, against the tide of those rushing downstream to hell. Normal is when you give demons headache and they incite hatred within people towards you. Normal is when you live a life that pleases God even when you're the only one in a million living that exact kind of life. That is my definition of normal.

That's precisely why Jesus remains my number one mentor and inspiration.

Look, the CNN news just showed clips of Jesus driving out the moneychangers. He is livid and throwing their stuff out. In a flowing white gown, long sandy brown hair and Roman sandals, he's tearing through the temple and they're screaming blue murder. According to the news report and an eyewitness account, 'There's a mad man on the loose. He's driving out drug pushers from the church. The magicians and money doublers have been kicked out as well.' In CNN language, that's probably what it would sound like.

The camera zooms in on Him and they sight the man shouting, 'This is my father's house, a house of prayer and not a den of thieves!' In a few seconds Twitter is buzzing, the pictures are all over Instagram, and Facebook is talking about Him. Even people who don't understand what's going on click 'like' on the post.

Something new is happening in the horizon. It's called 'Divine Norm.' This is when things happen just as Heaven planned them. It's when we let the kingdom of God rule and reign in our hearts and our lives such that it gets us noticed in Heaven. Once you settle for the world's definition of 'normal' you're sure to get it all wrong by God's standards. God's normal is not popular amongst mortals. Why do you want to be normal amongst mere mortals when you can be just like God? Ehen! Did that get your attention? That is God's original master plan for man. Remember Genesis? To 'make man in OUR image and likeness' not like some celebrity.

Funny thing about the norm is that it restricts you to this time and space. You have to do certain things at certain times because that's how it has always been. Joshua changed history by halting time in its journey. He commanded time to stand still. He dared the normal elements and reached to the elements of the world to come, because he understood who he was.

Let's break this down in layman's language. My dear friend is in her 40s and she's still single and a virgin. Ewwww, some people would say because by 10, and I kid you not, some kids are getting down and dirty. What!

You would say. Well, you're from the old school like me. That is atrocious right? Today, the piper plays the music differently than we used to know it. Life is evolving, they say, so anything goes. If I remember clearly, the word of God has stood the test of time and it NEVER EVER changes. God is the same now and forever. His standards stand sure and supreme.

Single at 40 is not the issue. Who said you have to have been at a certain place at a certain time doing a certain thing? What makes it normal? Because God defined it so or because people and perhaps medical science have pegged childbearing to a certain age?

When you choose the God path, please throw your thoughts of normal out the window. It will be so weird in heaven to act normal like the world. God's normal is the real normal.

Ponder this:

Do you sometimes wish you could just block everyone out and follow God blindly? You know, dare the norm and dare to be different? Actually, you can. He supplies the grace to be like Him. Just Do It.

4. Do You Like My Plaster?

Plaques on my wall
Testify of bravery,
Things I have done
Worthy of honour,
Tears in the dark
Only God knows,
His words of comfort
Like plasters to heal.
Come see my scars
Deep, dark and scaly,
Etched into my soul
To honour my King.

I made a very difficult phone call the other day. My hands trembled and my heart thumped wildly. I took in a deep breath to settle myself as I dialled. After a few minutes of emotion-laden conversation, she said to me, 'We cannot question God.' But my thoughts went, 'We dare not question God, if we mean serious business with Him.'

Remember as kids when we would try all manner of death defying stunts and come away with some bruises? Mum would wash the wound clean, apply some ointment and place some plaster(s) and tender kisses over it. We would go back out there to show our plaster off to everyone especially anyone who dared question our bravery. Sometimes we would even wish for bandages so that people would ask what happened and then we'd narrate how we fell down and hurt ourselves and bravely picked ourselves up. And then we'd get the stares of admiration, looks that told us we were the bravest thing ever. I know how we used to want a plaster on our arm or leg even when we were not hurt just so we could get that nod and compare with the other kids like a badge of honour. Do you like my plaster? How did you get yours? Well, I was riding my bike… And so the dialogue goes on.

Hmm. I sigh deeply as my mind returns to my friend. Her scar was the bereavement she had just endured, a time when she could have cursed God and died like Job's wife advised. She chose to hang in there instead. She chose to trust God. Everyone's scar is different. The place and timing is also peculiar to each and every one of us. Yours may barrel into your life early whilst some others may slip in much later in life. The constant thing though is that scars will be formed from trials and challenges of life. Crusted and healed, the scars will tell the tales you cannot tell. The scars will remain your badge of honour and the doorway to hoary hairs. Wisdom pursues people who have been through so much. There's always this settled look they have that points to years of endurance and triumph.

My friend understood the divine position on her challenge. She took to praise, which rather astounded me. She accepted her loss and she kept her face fixed on Jesus. From that moment on, I've had a high regard for the grace on her life. She was brutally wounded and that scar will remain a permanent reminder of her endurance. God's grace and comfort is like the plaster on her boo boo. She got a plaster. It's a sign of bravery.

'And ye have forgotten the exhortation which speaketh unto you as unto children, My son, despise not thou the chastening of the Lord, nor faint when thou art rebuked of him:' (Hebrews 12:5, KJV)

And when you have endured, there's a crown laid up for you (James 1:12).

Looking at the hall of fame in Hebrews 11:4-39, we see an imposing list of God's greats, men and women, ordinary by every means yet achieving great things for God. These were men and women who gave their entire lives in service to God and mankind. They suffered many things for the sake of the kingdom. Some were beheaded, sawn in two, boiled in oil and endured many other horrific things. Just like the child looks forward to the many kisses on their boo boo, they also would look forward to God's reckoning of their many scars one day.

Scars of war are highly commended. Veterans of war know this. You get a badge of honour for being in the war and of course extra recognition for surviving the war despite your many wounds. Veterans of war are highly recognized and honoured, more so in Heaven. There is not one disciple/apostle of Jesus, except Judas, who does not have a scar of life. Imagine walking through a line of saints in Heaven, heading to the majestic throne of God to get your crown. Reason? You endured all, you finished your race, and you didn't despise the persecutions, rejections, sufferings and the many things that gave you scars.

God will not only put a plaster on your boo boo, He will, like He did Jesus, give you a crown of glory. And you'll shout out, do you like my plaster?

Even Jesus endured the cross for the joy set before Him. (Hebrews 12:2).

Ponder this:

God loves those scars; the ones that make you like Jesus. Embrace them. In eternity they will be your badges of honour.

5. Peace Talks and God Listens

Deep within the heart
Where the running stream flows,
Every drop like words
Seeping deep inside,
Sighs above the hum
Should usher in stillness
So we can hear
God's whispers to us.

Isaac left off contending and dug another well. (Genesis 26:17-24)

He left two other wells and started all over again. That's something we need to consider. We can choose to leave off contentions and unfruitful connections and be ready to walk away from them.

Isaac dug a third well because he believed that he was prosperous. He knew God was with him even if he had to draw water from a stone. In other words, he turned the left cheek. Is it something you can do? Turn the left cheek? Walk away from palaver? Be an advocate for peace? Peace yields Sonship. **'Blessed are the peacemakers for they shall be called the children of God.' (Matthew 5:9, KJV)**

Consider this: God spins seeds in the dark until they sprout. It's dark, quiet and still where germination happens. God works best when you're still, when your heart is not troubled, because it's an indication that you trust Him.

Don't hope for a miracle in the midst of contention. It won't happen. Get away to a quiet place. You hear God best and you function best right there. And if it's a tornado that you can't control or stop, God will drop you in its eye and be with you as it churns furiously on the outside. Still your heart and life and neutralize every acidic connection. Acids erode. Pursue peace with all men, as much as you can. Choose to be the peacemaker in your family and sphere of influence. (Romans 12:18, Hebrews 12:14.) Pursue is an active word. It involves initiative, energy and enthusiasm.

When people make you rumble like a volcano and every conversation is like bubbly molten lava, you're headed for an explosion.

Personally, I don't like contentious people. I don't. I try as much as possible to be nice and sweet and friendly because I treasure peace and value my peace of mind. If I'm pushed to the wall, I'll roar back, but then you'd have to be pretty obnoxious to get me to that stage.

I know Cholerics can thrive in that atmosphere unfazed, because they can deal with the constant rush, but most of them don't mean any harm. They are just upbeat, that's all.

There's a difference between contentious/obnoxious people and people who are simply upbeat go-getters.

Note the difference and pick your battles.

Isaac didn't strive for God's blessing; he settled himself into it. It was his covenant right.

It was easy for God to reach out to him because he wasn't contentious, scheming, striving, grabbing and clawing at everything. He had every right to fight the people of Gerar for his father's well but he didn't.

Yet he grew until he became great. After he pursued peace, God appeared to him.

How do you hear from God anyway if you're all knotted up inside and cats and dogs are having a yelp party in your mind? Impossible is the word.

Don't rush around trying to put everyone in their place and all those things we do to re-assert our sense of self-importance and reinforce our no-nonsense stance.

Pursue peace first before you think of throwing the javelin. If you need to roar, roar at the devil. That's your real enemy anyhow. Jesus preached peace before He threw the moneychangers out and He wasn't fighting a personal cause. He was fighting a God cause. He exhibited holy anger.

And before you convince me that we sometimes exhibit holy anger, let me assure you that it's not as common as we think.

Let's be advocates for peace. Way above all the UN peace talks, only children of the Most High God can broker true peace.

We walk into our Sonship position when we stand for peace. There's a place for war and that's another story, but for today, peace is the umpire for the presence of God.

Ponder this:

When peace talks, God listens. What are you saying? Can you still hear Him? Are you listening?

6. Hands Up and Freeze

Let it go,
The timer you set
For answers to come
At your own time.
Let it go,
The reason you think
Plans will unfold
Your own way.
Let it go,
The way you imagine
God will come through.
Let it all go.

Yesterday, my daughter and I made a batch of ice-lollies. I painstakingly went through the process of helping her follow the recipe and preparation guidelines. You know, get her more involved to get me some respite from whining.

We poured the crushed pureed strawberry mulch into an ice-lolly mould and placed it in the freezer to wait the four-hour recommended freezing time.

We retired to the play area to watch TV. Five minutes into Sofia the First, my daughter asked if the lollies were ready. I shook my head. Another ten minutes later, she had asked half a dozen more times, by which time I had sighed, rolled my eyes, grumphed (blend of grumble and harrumph) and slumped my shoulders.

She wondered if sour, bruised, and crushed strawberries could really form ice-lollies. The idea that with a few added ingredients and a fancy mould, they could be solid and yummy, puzzled her.

Would they ever get solid, and why did it take so long were part of the next series of questions. Plus, she wanted me to check on them every second.

I took time to explain that the moment we mixed the right ingredients together we already made the lollies but the lollies still needed the right conditions to turn solid enough to have shape and be licked/sucked.

She took a few trips to the freezer to check on the lollies and often came back disappointed.

'Mummy, they're still soft and wobbly,' she would cry.

Even if it looks like a mess now, it still has the potential to fully assume the right shape.

I explained that the more she opened the freezer, the longer it would take for the lollies to set. In fact, the constant interruptions might prevent it from setting at all or it may develop ice crystals and then become slush rather than lollies.

Just like when we table our requests before God and we want to fast track the process through which the answer comes. It doesn't work like that.

Every fervent prayer needs the right conditions for fruition. Every seed needs the right conditions to germinate and grow. Life is in stages and the smooth transition of every stage needs the right conditions.

God takes His time to carefully watch over His word to perform it. (Jeremiah 1:12 AMP)

In other words, God is keenly interested in every stage of the development of the seed of His word. Every stage must reach its full potential and be perfect.

Every promise from God has inherent in it the capacity/ability 'TO BE', that is, to become whatever God says it should be.

Or perhaps you've set things in motion at the start of the year. You've prayed, planned and plotted, and you've set goals. You've got all the ingredients together. You've watered and planted. Now step back and let God give the increase.

Just like the lollies, you've got to HANDS UP and let it FREEZE. Be still and quietly wait. Quit meddling with it.

You can't rush this process. Certain divine conditions have to be in place. You've done your bit. Don't attempt to rush God through His bit. He does a perfect job all the time.

So relax, let God have His way. Timing is His specialty. He has never failed once and your case will not be an exception.

After a four-hour wait during which I had given a mini science lecture on the whys and where-to-fores of strawberries, just to distract her from further bombardments, we finally settled down to a good movie and yummy fruity ice-lollies. Slurp! Slurp! Yum! Praise God!

Ponder this:

Be patient. Be still. God is cooking something in His oven. He never disappoints. Always on point! Just wait, please.

7. Arise!

Arise,
Leave the past behind.
Arise,
And look up,
His promises to behold,
His gifts to bestow.
Arise
And see
Up is where you ought to be.

We got the ingredients: flour, yeast, water, some sugar, a pinch of salt, and a drizzle of oil.

We began the process of mixing it all together. We drowned the yeast with warm water and set aside to froth. We sifted flour and salt. Flour sprinkled everywhere like mounds of white dust. We made a well in the middle of the floury white hill and dumped the yeast mixture in.

We sweetened it with sugar and began to fiddle mix with our fingers.

We added a tiny dash of oil to ease friction in the stiff dough then placed it into a bowl. We wrapped it in a clean muslin cloth and placed it in an unlit oven to prove.

Thirty minutes later we pulled it out and gave it a whack to punch the air out because it had risen, but was not ready to be used. We rolled up our sleeves and began to work it. We kneaded, pulled, whacked, punched and kneaded again. It became soft, light and airy, yet not ready. We sent it back to the oven to prove one more time.

We need this bread to double in size. We have put all the ingredients and machinery in place to make it rise. It has to rise. It is expected.

Now imagine if after putting all the key ingredients in, we place the dough in the proving place and it doesn't rise; there'll be a problem. We wouldn't add more yeast. We would throw it away and start all over again.

We go through trials and temptations, but through it all God expects us to rise because of a key ingredient He put in us: Faith. Even faith as tiny as a mustard seed can move a mountain; just as a dash of yeast can double the size of dough. Faith in God's word is all you need to rise.

It's not the size of the seed, but the power in it. It's not even the trials or adversity but the fact that it's all leading us to the place where we can rise.

When we get whacked in the gut, rolled in mud, punched in the face and kneed in the groin, we can still rise up.

God doesn't throw us aside and start all over again with someone else because we refuse to rise after adversity crushes us. God keeps kneading and moulding us, never giving up, until we can rise up again.

The kneading hurts, the hot oven makes you howl, but they are just ingredients and steps to a new you. There's a certain je ne sais quoi that God put in us that makes us rise up, no matter what. We have to let the conditions align to make it work. So just rise up. You have what it takes. Our divine DNA is constituted to enable us rise and float above water.

After placing the 'risen' dough in the oven we waited to a gloriously soft and yummy loaf of homemade bread, with butter waiting in the wings. Yummy!

Ponder this:

Make it happen! Get up! God is behind you. His arms will bear you up and give you wings to fly. You just have to arise! Do you think you can? Yes, you can!

8. The Blind Spot

We all are blind to see
What's before and behind us,
Although we claim to see
What steps we often take
Whilst others see
Where we have not been.
Yet when we look back,
We see what we blindly
Did not see before.

No matter how good a driver you are, there will always come a time when a car from the rear slips onto your blind spot.

It happens often and only seasoned drivers will double-check before they pull onto an adjacent lane. Checking the rear-view mirror or the side mirror will not often yield a view of the car in the 'blind spot'. The blind spot is that invisible place between the side mirror and the rear-view mirror where you don't see the oncoming car. Search me, I'm a woman and I am clueless as to why, neither can I explain the mechanics behind the blind spot. All I know is that when changing lanes, I am often conscious of the blind spot, so I don't pull out in front of a speeding car and cause an accident.

Did you know that people also slip into our blind spot? The blind spot is that place where we are oblivious of them and their intentions. It's that place where we could be secretly disliked, misjudged, misunderstood or even hated. And we don't even know what we did wrong. The blind spot is that place where we could have stepped on someone's toes, said something nasty without thinking, or reacted wrongly to a situation. And these actions incur someone's wrath; that is the offended party. A friend could be seething with ire while you carry on as though you're still on good terms. They've been in your blind spot and you didn't know. Perhaps over a period of time, this misunderstanding deepens, and fosters hatred and ill feelings. It destroys relationships and if two people were to sit down and go back to the root cause of the problem, it's always a case of misunderstandings or miscommunication that stemmed from a petty matter.

Sometimes, we never get a chance to right the wrongs caused by the blind spot. Sometimes we are too myopic to think beyond the front of our nose. Has it ever happened to you? Of course you'd nod in the affirmative. People slip into our blind spot, we pull out without checking and then wham, we collide with them. Sometimes we don't collide. It's a near miss and we carry on, leaving behind someone who'd had to slam on his or her brakes just to avoid collision. While we speed off, they're mad as hell, shaking their fist at the plumes of dust left behind by our car.

The only way out of a blind spot is to triple check. Be conscious and considerate of other drivers on the road. Don't make assumptions and don't take anything for granted. Check and check again before you pull out.

Just as in driving, the way out of the human blind spot is to slow down a bit. Don't run roughshod over other people. As much as you can, be considerate. Sometimes you can't help who lurks around your blind spot and sometimes you end up in someone else's blind spot. Whatever the case may be, do what you can to take care of your blind spot. If however, the blind spot is indeed invisible to you as will be on many occasions, don't sweat it. Let life run its due course. When you have ample opportunity and people emerge out of your blind spot, embrace them. In so doing you make it obvious you were previously oblivious.

The blind spot is as common to life as breathing. There will always be someone in your blind spot, and you will always be in someone's blind spot. As the saying goes, 'To err is human.' We will err from time to time. We need to cut ourselves some slack as we do others.

Live conscious of others. You never know who might emerge from your blind spot and be your escort or pacesetter.

Ponder this:

Can you please be a little patient? Someone might be caught in your blind spot. Give room so they can emerge. Please be patient.

9. I Don't Wanna Be Special

Although I want to be like others,
Living the same kind of life,
Living off of promises
Life serves them daily
Forgetting about my place,
Trading it for mundane,
Refusing to see
Diamonds though
Gleaming in the rough
Are often destined
For the throne in the palace.

My little princess loves to dress up. She has her couture moments. This season might be pants, whilst the other might be a dress. It just depends on whatever takes her fancy. I have learned to flow in her seasons otherwise it would be a never-ending battle of wits.

And speaking of wits, lately she had begun to rescind on her seasonal preferences. She would want to wear something just because a friend wore the same thing. I remember borrowing a line that she needn't be like everyone. She asked me why and I responded, 'because you're special.'

She simply nodded, scrunched her forehead in thought and resumed putting on the said dress that was the crux of our argument. I assumed she understood what I meant when I said she needn't dress up like everyone else or be like other people. I reminded her to consider changing her clothes.

She hunched her shoulders, then looked up and said: 'But mummy, I don't wanna be special. I wanna be just like everyone else.' In other words, I wanna fit in and flow and invariably be liked rather than ridiculed.

The bells rang in my head. A deja vu moment hit me. The children of Israel wanted to be like everyone else. They wanted a human king, not God as king. They too did not want to stick out like a sore thumb. How did God feel about that? Maybe like I'm feeling right now. Frustrated and wishing Lil Princess would just get it.

As Christians there seem to be certain rules and invisible boundaries guiding our lives. There are certain things we cannot do, certain people we cannot mix with and certain places we daren't go. The people of the world always seem to be free to be and do whatever they like while we cannot.

It can be frustrating without understanding why we are different. They seem to be happy and getting on with their lives. In fact, they always appear happy. At the season when we have to be on a fast is when the new disco joint happens down the road. All night we hear celebratory screams and happy shouts, while we have to stay indoors to pray and read the scriptures.

It usually looks that way on the surface, far above the depths where the reality of sorrows and depression lies.

Yet the gates that seem like barriers actually keep us safe. The enemy is always prowling around waiting for those to eat up.

Permit me to digress a little. Have you ever heard of the man who seemed to have it all: fame, fortune, power and just about everything that can ever fulfil a man? You have, huh? On the news right about the same time I watched. So why did he commit suicide? Can you imagine that? He had everything most people desire, yet he committed suicide, leaving all his acquired wealth behind.

What do you think went wrong? It's been the same story really. Despite having it all, something always seems to be missing. Admit it or not, that God-created vacuum can never be filled by things or other people. It was never meant to be.

As long as we try to fill that vacuum with anything other than God we will never find true joy, fulfilment or satisfaction.

God was doing a mighty fine job leading His people through His desired method before they started craving for a king like everyone else. Read through the scriptures. Whilst they were clamouring for a king, other nations held the Israelites in high esteem and were terrified of them because of the way God fought for them. The 21st-century church is pretty much like the children of Israel. We want the best of both worlds. We want to be like the world whilst in church. We don't want to be different. We don't want to be special. We crave love and acceptance by people almost at any cost when we're already loved and accepted by God.

I know it's typical. We all want to be loved and accepted by people. Certainly, nobody wants to walk alone or be termed weird just because we're different. But God always has a bigger and better plan than our imagination can handle. Trust me, you want to be on the side of the One who holds the world in the palm of His hand.

Even when my daughter dresses to be like others, she cannot run to them when she's in trouble. She would run to me at the drop of a hat. She trusts me. To me she will always be special. I always pray that she will come to realise it, just as God waits for us to understand and embrace the fact that we are already 'SPECIAL'.

Ponder this:

Do you sometimes wish you were like everyone else, doing what everyone else is doing? Do you think it is tedious trying to be different for God? God understands, but He has grand plans for our today and tomorrow. You are special to God. Be the special God wants you to be.

10. How Long Will You Mourn?

Don't mourn
Because of changes.
Don't mourn
Because of detours.
Look for the light
At the tunnel's end.
Focus only on
Your finish line.

It's 6:45am and I am in the middle of Bible study/devotion. I have a lot going on in my mind. I feel the need to journal on my blog. I feel weighed down by so many things; things like how I take my daily walk with God or how to live in continual victory one day at a time.

In one of my mini Ebooks, **LightBulb Musings**, there's a chapter about reviewing our connections.

I admit that I am one to make very slow connections and once I do, I must have a very good reason to let go. I'm not the clingy type friend. I love my space and would give that too in return. I could never make a besto these days. It's hard to keep up with life, talk less of having to keep up with one particular friend. However, I love and respect all the connections in my life. Like I said, I don't make them easily.

I finished editing the new mini book and I got stuck on the chapter that talked about reviewing your connections because it spoke to me.

What do you do when a connection becomes toxic? I have come to realise that communication is the number one problem in a lot of connections. By connection in this instance, I'm talking mainly about friendship. Once there's breakdown in communication a lot is left unsaid and therefore a lot is assumed to be said that wasn't even said.

If we really, truly were interested in a connection we would make the effort to meet half way, and open up discussions to resolve issues. That's what is expected of a vibrant connection; i.e. people who both value the friendship and desire to stay connected. On the other hand, when the intention is not to pursue an amendment but rather to lay blame, or when the breakdown is as a result of one person wanting to have their way and becoming cantankerous when they don't, it's a sign of a controller and an abuser. You need to be in shuffle mode and shuffle yourself out of there as fast as you can.

I am afraid for people who hold on longer than necessary to a relationship they have no business being in. It's a sign of a low self-worth to feel you absolutely need some people in your life.

You will and can survive without them. I am afraid of people who act like they are God and nobody can live without them. Nobody is indispensable. Everyone is replaceable. When my mum died, I thought I could never live without her, never have a normal life again. I did a lot of things out of fear to preserve her memory. Today, with God's help I am living without her. I miss her terribly but God has been my mainstay. It's liberating when God is the only one you cannot live without.

I am afraid of people who make themselves look like you need them and your life is worth nothing without them or their input. Hmmmm! They don't know God. That's why. God can snuff them out with a blink and replace them in a heartbeat.

The Lord taught me many years ago to periodically review my connections, and I have often been reluctant to. Now I fully understand why. I am embarking on another cleansing ritual. I will be disconnecting from connections that are not just toxic but are pursuing a different path from mine. You need to as well if you will move on with God to the next level.

It's not a sentimental decision. It should be a carefully orchestrated divine decision. It should be made prayerfully. Let God bring people your way when and how and for how long He desires to. Don't hold on to a toxic relationship when God is clearly moving on.

Remember what God said to Samuel: How long will you mourn for Saul seeing I have rejected him? There's David waiting in the wings, why mourn for Saul?

'And the Lord said unto Samuel, How long wilt thou mourn for Saul, seeing I have rejected him from reigning over Israel? fill thine horn with oil, and go, I will send thee to Jesse the Beth–lehemite: for I have provided me a king among his sons.' (1 Samuel 16:1, KJV)

Let go and let God bring fruitful connections your way. David was a sterling king. From his lineage came the Messiah. Don't short-change yourself by holding on to something when God has better things in store for you.

Ponder this:

Are you one of those extremely sympathetic people who want to explain every relationship when God is telling you to let go? Letting go doesn't mean you hate. It simply means you're going in a different direction and two cannot walk together unless they agree. So do let go.

11. The King, Moses and Noah Were Left Behind

God runs His own commentary
In the Bible.
His words
In the Bible,
His thoughts
In the Bible,
His feelings
In the Bible too.

I haven't sat down to watch TV in ages. I think being forced to stay at home for an entire weekend due to the national elections made me remember we had a TV. I'm usually very selective of what I watch. My TV/movie viewing is predictable. When I do watch TV at all, it's sure to be comedy, food network or Christian TV. That's all. Once in a while I could do the action/thriller/mystery combo as long as there's no blood or gore.

I pre-set the timings for a marathon show and settled myself down to watch three movies that I thought would be interesting. Thinking back to the torture I put myself through, I groan out loud.

First up was ***Noah***. My question is this: Has Hollywood run out of scripts or movies to make? This movie called ***Noah*** was nothing short of a fantasy movie, because to write about or depict otherworldly events, you have to fantasize. The only resemblance this movie has with the Bible is the name ***Noah*** and the ark that looked more like a sinister floating alcove hiding googly-eyed monsters. The emphasis of course was not on the message. They had no message to preach anyway. The emphasis was not on God either. I presume my readers have read the story of Noah in the Bible. When I saw humongous reptiles sliding their way towards the ark, I reached for my remote control and conveniently searched for the food network channel.

When I discussed this movie with a few people who were brave enough to watch till the end I almost puked. Apparently, it was said, written and acted out, that fallen angels helped *Noah* to build and complete the ark. What utter nonsense! The message therefore was that the fallen angels have earned their redemptive rights. Why can't Hollywood just write scripts about the world they know or other perceived worlds rather the Bible world? The world is crazy enough as it is with 'stranger than fiction' events to fill many books. Why delve into unknown territory? The Bible is God's word and not Space 1999, going to worlds never known or conquered before.

The whole idea is to contaminate the minds of people, twist the truths of the Bible, and further desensitize people —— especially unsuspecting Christians —to the real deal. They attempt to make a mockery of the word of God with the hope of driving people further away by sensationalizing and dramatizing falsehood. Or perhaps the story of *Noah* makes for a good movie and it's not about honouring the Bible.

I thought *Noah* was bad then I switched over to *Left Behind*, the movie adapted from Jerry B. Jenkins and Tim LaHaye's *Left Behind* series. I read the first ten books in the series when they were first published. After the tenth book, I got bored and left reading. I am very familiar with the entire story especially since it is based on the Bible. I didn't get to watch the one acted by Christians, aired on TBN, but when this one came up I thought it couldn't be that bad. It started out all well and good. The rapture and the explosive aftermath were quite dramatic. Thereafter, it went downhill. They tried to build an entire movie on the rapture and right after the rapture they ran out of things to say or do.

Now if this movie had a solid Christian background and scripting backed up by Hollywood's mega millions, I think we might have gotten close to getting a good balance of the message and the drama. Again, emphasis was not really on God or the Bible. It was inferred, but not focused on. The whole scenario came across like two bored teenagers trying to act out or depict their thoughts of the rapture using animation and graphics pasted on real human beings. Why can't Hollywood just leave the Christian version alone? We've read the Bible, and the book that inspired the story. Some of us have seen the movie acted out by Christians. That's good enough for us. This movie is not all that bad. A non-Christian can watch the movie and be moved to the Lord. That can absolutely happen, but yet again, I question the motive behind the making of the movie when the people who understand the story better had already made one.

Finally, and the mother of them all, is ***Gods and Kings***. I was intrigued by the modern version of the ***Ten Commandments***. With this movie I had my antennas up. I was ready for the worst and my predictions were so true. First of all, the Rameses looked pathetically weak. Not the same stubborn goat described in the Bible. This one was weak and foolish and he couldn't even fight in a battle.

The storyline was grossly compromised. The burning bush was the determining factor. The bush was a tiny shrub that merely threw sparks of fire here and there. And then God? This was for me the most humiliating part. God was depicted as a little eight-year-old boy who simply told Moses to return to Egypt. Moses went back to Egypt and started training the children of Israel to fight with swords, etc. Yet we know that the freeing of the Israelites from Egypt was a purely supernatural act. Nothing less.

And here's when I almost stopped watching. The Red Sea did not part. It slowly ebbed and the people waded in waist high water. What? That didn't happen. Show me where it happened that way in the Bible. That's why I say Hollywood should mind their business and go look for fantasy on planet Neptune and leave the Bible and its interpretation to us. We're satisfied with how God illuminates our minds with the truth. And if they must act out the Bible they should consult the experts.

And there you have it. My groaning moments watching what I thought would be blockbusters. I encourage Christians to please get so familiar with the Bible that you can spot a false doctrine a mile away. The enemy is out to dilute the truth. The Bible did say that in the last days, the truth would be scarce. Determine to search for the truth and live for the truth.

Ponder this:

Do you watch and read circumspectly? You should. The devil craftily plants lies through everything to shift the truth and make us compromise. Don't buy the lie. Search the word. The truth is in it.

12. The Pringle Martyr

Weeping that night,
Kneeling to pray,
Where hours He groaned,
Losing His sleep,
Was what He did
To give His life
For you and me,
That we may live.

I was knackered, but I had to pick my daughter up from school. On our way back, I made a quick stop at the corner shop to get something I had promised her the day before as reward for good behaviour.

We walked down the aisle and she picked her prized to-be possession: two green tubs of Pringles. Excitement was written all over her face as she hopped over to the till and handed in the purchase to the cashier.

As she handed over the cash I had given her, I noticed a young man watching us intently from one corner of the shop.

He walked up to me and said "hello Ma. Is this all you came to get at the supermarket," he raised his eyebrows, 'two tubs of Pringles?"

I smiled and nodded.

'Wow! That's some sacrifice.'

'Really?' I replied.

I hadn't thought of it that way until he mentioned the fact. I was taken somewhat aback. Was it the fact that I had promised my daughter that I would reward her for good behaviour or was it that fact that I loved the look of sheer delight on her face when she paid for the Pringles? For whichever of the two and perhaps even more reasons, I didn't quite see the sacrifice in what I did. I just thought it was an act of love.

'Yup,' he retorted, 'that's why I'm not getting married in a hurry.'

I think at this point the only word I could roll off my tongue was 'Really?'

Still, I needed clarity. What did he mean? What was I missing? I'm a mother. I don't know how to not think like one. Mother's sacrifice. It's nature-made.

'Excuse me?'

He turned to regard me.

'Yup,' he smirked, 'Not having kids at all."

I stared at him for a while, hardly blinking.

'You don't want to have kids because you don't want the privilege of birthing a life?'

He shifted his stance and rocked from one foot to another. I ignored his discomfort and plowed on. 'Or you don't want kids because you can't give yourself to another, have an interrupted life, shape a destiny, a generation, a nation?'

My dear young man looked like he would take a flight any moment now. I stopped in my tracks when I realized I probably was going too far. What did it matter; it was just two measly tubs of Pringles. I wasn't upset or anything. On the contrary I was just wondering if we truly understand the word 'sacrifice' or not.

Rather than dwell on the word 'sacrifice' I would rather dwell on the word 'love'. Love is not a cliché. It's what we do for those we love that some call sacrifice. For God 'so loved' the world that He 'gave' life. (Paraphrase mine) God's goal was to express His love for us even though it cost Him so much.

The trip to the store up a flight of steps, with me panting, just to get Pringles for my daughter might have felt like a hassle but that look of pure delight and oh that smile, blew all my fatigue away. Really and truly I didn't see it as a sacrifice. I thought it was an act of love.

Everything God does is an act of love despite the great sacrifice behind it all. He did it all just for you and me. Isn't that a great and comforting thought?

Ponder this:

Do you feel afraid to love, to give your all to another? Love is actually what makes life meaningful and beautiful. Love never fails. You can never fail loving. Jesus didn't and neither will you.

13. Gossip With My Daddy

Let's share our secrets
Then lock them up
Make them safe and secure
In a vault with bolts,
Safe from prying eyes
And tattletales.
Let's place them
Right before the Lord
Who keeps secrets best of all.

Social media is stripping away privacy. It's all part of the mega ploy to usher in the one world government. That means you daren't air your secrets in public all in the name of socializing without a boomerang effect. Wisdom dictates prudence with our words on social media. No online personality is to be trusted explicitly. However, you know you can trust God with your secrets. Whom will He need to tell anyway?

Thus went my train of thought when my daughter informed me she would tell her Dad some secret of hers. She tells her Dad everything. The time of the event is immaterial; she'd stay up late just to recount teensy-weensy details to her dad: what, when, how, where and with whom. Her father is her main confidant.

Do you have a most trusted confidant besides God?

God wants to be confided in. That we can confide in God, tell Him our deepest darkest secrets and problems, sometimes eludes us. Wouldn't God disapprove of our most sincere yet bizarre and often sinful thoughts? How can we share that with a most Holy God? That we got jealous of someone or envious and really angry to the point of wanting to shoot them? Or even that we're disappointed in God over how He either didn't answer our prayers or didn't deliver the type of results we hoped for? How can we bare our hearts and soul to God? Can you stomach the thought? Yet we report God to people as though there could ever be a fairer or more just God, or there could ever be an advocate for us, against God.

God is actually easier to live with than we realize. He loves us infinitely despite His hatred for sin. Perhaps through David's life we can get a little glimpse of God. David is one man who found his way into God's heart. Despite his obvious below the belt sins, he manages to capture God's heart. He's sincere and quick to repent. That's what God finds endearing about him.

Some of us talk to God, complain to Him, demand stuff from Him or even harass Him. When was the last time you 'talked' with God? I mean a back and forth banter. Not a table your request and then leave the vicinity kind of chat.

We talk 'with' God through worship and adoration, through pouring our heart out and being willing to wait to hear from Him. It takes time to get acquainted with His voice in response to our voice. He loves to chat with us. You can tell Him anything. He's the wisest and most understanding confidant there ever will be. He's not judgmental. He's not cynical or pretentious. He really does have your interest at heart. He doesn't half listen; He listens wholeheartedly. He has the solution to your problem; the answer to your question. He will never broadcast your deepest secrets to another when you confide in Him your struggles and your pain. He's therefore the best person to 'gist' with and tell it all. He loves to gist, do you know? He loves when you sit at His feet and just gist with Him. He loves you, His gist partner. He loves you endlessly.

Ponder this:

If you don't understand God at all, understand this: God loves you. He is loving... oh so loving. I kid you not. He's as loving, merciful and beautiful for every situation.

14. A Being Called Me

Jesus loves you
Do you know?
Check the Bible
You'll find out so.
Yes Jesus loves you,
Read the story
In His word;
It's all about
His love for you.

'I will praise thee; for I am fearfully and wonderfully made: marvellous are thy works; and that my soul knoweth right well.' (Psalm 139:14, KJV)

Do you believe you'd be happier being someone else? Do you ever feel others are accomplishing wonderful things while you feel invisible, unappreciated and or feel like you're achieving nothing? Do you ever get envious of other richer, prettier, wittier people? Have you ever felt all the troubles of the world are targeted at you? Have you ever asked 'why me?' or secretly felt sorry for yourself? Well, I have good news for you, you're not here as a part of a package of rejects catapulted to earth. The Creator and Master-Planner of the universe had you in mind — your very essence, nature, character, personality, weaknesses, shortcomings and all — when He formed you in your mother's womb. Let me assure you that He took His time fashioning you to accomplish great things.

We very often feel inadequate because we don't have a pointy nose combined with an hourglass figure or we don't look like Miss or Mr World. Other times we feel insecure, wishing we had more money, more education, worked in a blue-chip company or were simply tagged famous or successful. On the flip side, we secretly judge others in our hearts, wondering why they don't look like we do, talk like we do or simply be like us just so we don't feel bad about ourselves. Make no mistake, God didn't create clones. Every time you try to be somebody else, you short-change yourself and delay your destiny. This is not about re-inventing the wheel but finding your unique be-ing (not selling) point.

There are very many people who wish they were somebody else; richer, more successful, prettier, more educated, and the list goes on. In our quest to fill in our inadequacies, we add more honorary degrees, prop up the saggy body bits, or correct features God loving crafted. Yes, even that fat, spread-out nose was lovingly crafted by God. One day we shall shed this mortal body and it wouldn't matter then if we were white, black, pretty, ugly, skinny, short or dumpy.

Sometimes we don't let people get to know the real us because we are afraid they will discover something about us that they won't like. Or we try to pull back from them because we fear that they've already found something distasteful and will reject us. That cannot happen with God. He knows us completely and still He accepts and loves us.

And of course there are situations where people can hardly do anything about how they see themselves or feel about themselves. It could stem from a nasty childhood resulting in low self-worth, abusive relationships and the like. The truth is that only God can re-define people with scars from their past. If the Holy Spirit is allowed to work in them, they would see and appreciate their value and worth.

The entire human race is on a race to prove themselves to the world; to prove that they matter. The issue of acceptance is deeply rooted in most of our pursuits. We showcase our talents, our good looks, our eloquence or gift of the garb, our knowledge of deep things and the list goes on. The truth is that everything we are and hope to be was created or given to us by

God. So really how we feel about ourselves should not be solely dependent on what we possess or don't possess. God didn't consult us when He chose to love us; therefore our self-image should be based on what we already are, 'fearfully and wonderfully made'.

Our looks, talents, gifts, cultural background, familial background and everything that defines us were carefully chosen by God. If He deemed it necessary to make us white, we would be white, born rich or poor, educated or not. Our situation is certainly not a mistake by God. He planted us where we are, made us who we are in order to fulfill a purpose. If Jacob understood this fact, he wouldn't need to be so manipulative and conniving. It had to take God breaking his strength before he finally understood he was already chosen.

The only way out of an insecure, self-analytic and self-centred life is to go back to our God and find out who you really are and what you're here on earth to accomplish. No man can define you, not even the most coveted affluent position on earth; only God. When Jacob finally realized who He was, he stopped chasing shadows and finally rested, knowing that God would lead him to his promised land. When you discover who you are in Christ, you'd be energized and too occupied learning and preparing for your calling to notice or care about other people's opinion of your worth.

In Psalm 139:14, 'I will praise thee; for I am fearfully and wonderfully made: marvellous are thy works; and that my soul knoweth right well,' we are reminded of the fact that we are of tremendous value in God's eyes. God's character goes into the creation of every person therefore we should have as much respect for ourselves as our Maker has for us.

Psalm 139 is a celebration of a wonderful relationship; that of a close friend –God. God knows us better than our closest confidant— even better than we know ourselves— yet He loves and accepts us the way we are and is willing to work in and through us to make us the kind of people He wants us to be. (Matt 10:30).

When you fear (or actually face) rejection from others—whether co-workers, neighbours, friends, or even family members—remember that God made you and has already accepted you, exactly as you are. For this reason we ought to shout and give praise to Him for we have been wonderfully made and are deeply loved.

I for one believe I am deeply loved by God and am therefore a gift to the world. What about you?

Ponder this:

A loving God unequivocally loves you. Have you accepted that truth? You should.

15. Madame Bovary, Dine Not

They said to use a long fork
When dining with the enemy
Of whose meal will it be?
Or whose plate will it be?
Or whose place is it at?
And who then is deceived?
For the matter is not to dine
But whom you're dining with.

Madame Bovary wasn't a book I delighted in reading back then in the University. It was intriguing yet tedious. I didn't quite fancy the old English translated from the French language. I don't know how to express it but it's all that rolled in one. Sometime ago I stumbled on Madame Bovary on my IBook reader and decided to take it on a reading spin. Well, well, well, did I see things that I never saw before! I am technically almost three decades away from the last time I read it, so maturity should dictate I see things anew.

Summary: Madame Bovary had her head in the clouds thinking marriage is all romance like in novels. Imagine the shock she got when she married a 'boorish' doctor who had no imagination beyond tending to patients and dispensing drugs.

She was going to fix that. She hooked up with Rodolphe, a dashing young man, to have the wildest and most romantic moments of her life and perhaps elope with him. Rodolphe of course had no intention of doing that so on the night to elope, he stood her up.

After a few weeks of being heartbroken she dove back into the dating scene, having clandestine meetings with another young man. He also dropped her after a few weeks. She'd been dumped twice and ran up a huge bill from buying clothes and things she thought would make her happy and keep the men interested.

Oh the shame! She decided to end it all. She drank an overdose of the opium, Laudanum and never woke up. Her husband, oblivious to all her misdeeds, was devastated. One day he ran into Rodolphe, the erstwhile lover of his late wife. Although initially startled, when Rodolphe realised that Charles was in the dark about what went down with his wife, he invited Charles to drink with him.

And they became drinking buddies until the day Charles stumbled upon love letters exchanged between his late wife and Rodolphe. Another pain engulfed him. The next time he met up with Rodolphe he stared at the man with full knowledge of who he was.

Charles had been dining with the enemy and he was clueless. The enemy liked his identity to remain hidden so that he could have full access into his life without having to stanch his guilt. Rodolphe almost got away with it.

That's precisely how the devil works. He wants his real identity and intention hidden so he can dine with you. He doesn't even mind if you think he doesn't exist. He robes himself in all the multi-religious cults of the world to entice people into believing they are seeking their own way to God. His true intention is to lure people from the real and only way to God; through Jesus. He's that crafty. Yet he's no match for our God.

Sometimes we dine with people whose real identity we are yet to figure out. We think they're friends while they see us as prey, fodder for whatever nonsensical scheme they have up their sleeve.

As you plan your life and embark on new journeys and thresholds, mind whom you dine with. Not everyone who says 'friend' is really that to you. On the flipside don›t go witch hunting. The real enemy is the devil, but he uses people to achieve his goals.

Let God choose and direct your steps so you don't dine with the enemy.

Ponder this:

You dine with people you wish to spend quality time with. You dine with God, not the enemy. It's not the crockery that matters. It's whom you dine with that's in question. Dine with God and live.

16. Believe a Single Story

His story
Is the foundation of the world.
His story
Is the story of you and me.
His story
Contains all the truths.
His story
Is the only single story there is.

Years ago when I took a class at the University, the lecturer informed us that it would be better, if we were Christians, to drop a particular course we were about to sign up for and take another. He gave a reason. The reason was that the book we were to read was written by the devil. Yikes!

I won't be tempted to tell you the name of the book. It's not that important. However, here's the thing: I was a newbie Christian. I had just received Christ into my heart a month prior. I hadn't even fully grasped the truths of God's words. I was still in a diaper so to speak.

But I was curious. What story could the devil write that would entice me to go back to the dark side? I needed to know. For some reason I wasn't afraid of being lured away. Many of my classmates who were Christians dropped the course. When I saw that my mentor at the time stayed put, it was all the impetus I needed to do the same.

Yes it was a silly book and I wasn't the least bit convinced of the argument it put forth. It started with these lines: You have heard God's side of the story in the Bible. Why don't you hear the other side of the story? Then you can be the judge.

Wowzers! That's mighty tempting isn't it? Well, yes we read the story and had to pass the exam for the story. Imagine that!

I didn't need the devil's side of the story to know whose side I should be on. I didn't need another witness or story from the other side. Where God is concerned I don't need another side. There can't be another side. Who's going to stand and be on the other side against God?

I choose to believe a singular story; God's story. God honours His word above His name (Psalm 138:2). What He tells me in His word is sufficient for me. I don't need another angle or another story. Why? Because I believe in God. He's a loving and faithful Father and He loves me infinitely.

Will you also believe His singular story that who He says He is, He is? What He says He will do/perform, He will.

Ponder this:

God has never failed. His methods are not human and cannot be comprehended except by the heart, your spirit. God honours His words even above His name. He is the real deal. Trust Him. Believe His single story. There's no other.

17. The Hint Button

God hints
of His plans,
God hints
Of your part.
Press the hint button,
He wants to show you destiny.

Awhile ago when we chatted my sister mentioned something about the steps we take and where they lead us in life. The choices we make determine whether we walk with a spring in our step, or our steps are drudgery; whether our steps are directed or haphazard.

Watching my daughter lay on the hospital bed wasn't something I liked. No mother would. It was a hot and humid day and I had been up all night, watching and waiting, sponging her down with a cool damp towel. If I could pour a bucket load of ice on her and get the temperature down, I would do it in a flash and tame the raging fever. Sleep deprived and feeling all cranky, I scrolled through my Samsung phone and landed on the Playstore App. Since the days of Dell desktop games, I hadn't seen the likes of the game Solitaire. I hadn't played Solitaire in more than a decade. I was done biting my nails and chewing my lip. I clicked download and watched the green stream of the app loading itself on my screen and taking up residence in a corner.

I smiled as I clicked on Solitaire. My favourite game style is the Vegas scoring style. Why do I like it? Simple. It's difficult and you hardly ever win. Suits me just fine. I'd be bored if it were any easier. As I played this game to kill time, my daughter woke up and got all interested in what I was engrossed in staring at my phone as though I was calculating millions.

I told her about the game and then taught her how to play it. I'd adjusted the game to the easy and basic scoring style. After a few attempts she got frustrated and almost gave up. I kept encouraging her to keep at it and use her brains. That kept her quiet for a while, plus it gave her something to do rather than stare at the bag of IV infusion dangling above her head. I got busy with my iPad reading a book on my Kindle. It wasn't long before I stopped hearing her huffs, puffs and sighs of frustration. I wondered if she had mastered the game already. I couldn't put that past her techie generation.

Then she whooped for joy. She'd won her first game and then the next and many more after that. I was curious. How did she learn to win so quickly? What was her secret? I found out that she used the 'hint' button a lot. The hint button tells her where the next move is. That was her secret. It's not a cheat button but a hint button. It was put there to help you when you're stuck. She used the hint button and made playing the game not only fun but also easy to solve. She chose to do things that way. It worked for her and all was well.

I didn't give the episode another thought until my sister made that statement about the steps that we take and how they can be directed by God or self-directed. Hmmm, I got thinking.

How do we tread in life? When we want to take a step do we simply take whatever steps we fancy or do we pause and get a hint?

The next day, when her condition did not improve, I took my daughter home from the neighbourhood clinic with the intention to take her to the family clinic for a second opinion. I got her overnight bag and began tossing her stuff inside when the Holy Spirit stopped me in my tracks and asked if I wanted her to go back to stay at the hospital. I definitely did not. I had prayed for direction earlier and then made a decision to go for a second opinion. Because I had asked for a 'hint' of what to do, I got stopped in my tracks. I left the overnight bag behind. After a visit with the family doctor I didn't need to keep my daughter overnight at the clinic after all. I got a 'hint' from the Lord that I wouldn't need to. She was going to get better.

How about if we got a 'hint' about what steps we take so that we don't go places that might lead us to a dead end? How about if we often rely on the leading of the Holy Spirit so that as we chart the course of each day, week, month and year we get to go in the direction we ought to and save ourselves from unnecessary detours? It makes the journey easier and more sensible than groping around in the dark. Another way is to have seasoned mentors who can give us a 'hint' which way to go so we don't have to make unnecessary and avoidable mistakes as we go along the route of life. Imagine the burnout Moses would have endured had Jethro, his father-in-law, not come to the rescue (Exodus 18).

Imagine starting the year with a blueprint or a hint of what God wants to accomplish in and through us? What happens then is that our pathway becomes streamlined. We don't dart here and there or aim blindly. We shoot sharp because we have a 'hint' in what direction we should be headed. It simply makes life much more targeted at success. Life becomes much more sensible and kingdom focused when we get a hint of tomorrow, not from a tarot card but from God Himself who owns tomorrow.

Ponder this:

We get 'hints' through His words. We get 'hints' when we pray. We get 'hints' in His presence. Don't you want to get 'hints' for your life? Get God.

18. Step On and Start

Start with God
Cruise in your lane
Run your race
Finish your course
Get your prize.

I had a plan. I had to. The flab crept everywhere around my frame. I had pushed beyond the BMI boundary. The medics recommended specified workouts. Some workouts would transform the flab to fab while the others not recommended could 'testosteronify' me. We wouldn't want people confused about my gender now would we? I'm not flying a transgender kite. At. All.

So off to the gym I went. I donned my sweat attire, snatched my keys, jumped in the car and drove down to the sweat room. I held my breath at the beautiful sight before me. Machines of different colours, shapes and sizes performing all manner of magic to people. Machine to tone this and bulk that. These machines targeted different parts of the anatomy. You couldn't just jump on any without understanding its function and how well suited it is for you and your specific needs.

I had my instruction card with me. In spite of the excitement of seeing all the machines, I didn't need them all. I needed some for certain functions.

After speaking with my gym instructor, I settled down and got ready to roll. I stepped on the machine and he depressed the green button. He set my age, current weight, duration, desired workout speed and level, and then the start button. Then I began pounding the pavement. It wasn't easy at first. I thought my heart was going to give up, never mind that I started at the lowest setting ever. I was panting. I signalled to the gym instructor. He rolled his eyes and assured me, after many protests, that I was right on course. He urged me to keep going until I broke sweat and the sweat trailed a sizeable map on my top. Breaking sweat wasn't as easy as I thought. That first day was the hardest. I broke no sweat. I kept willing the sweat to come out. Imagine that! Meanwhile if the electric company were to cut off electricity at home, I'd be sweating in no time. And here I was trying to sweat at all cost. Sweat apparently means I'm doing something worthwhile.

By day five, I knew my settings and didn't need help customizing the machine just for me. Two weeks later, sweat and I became companions. I just had to wiggle a bit and sweat would gush out, too happy to see me. So we cheerfully went along with the programme.

No distractions. That is until the day someone stepped on the machine beside me and asked if it was okay for her to use it because she'd been watching me for a while and she liked my sweat factor. She also liked the machine beside mine, which was similar to what I currently used. The question then was, if it could work magic for me, why not her? I thought it was odd, but then again I guessed being polite was not a bad thing. I nodded okay.

She quickly glanced at my settings and set her machine to my settings. She then plunked on the machine and began doing her thing. For a while she smiled and mouthed to me from the mirror in front of us, what I assumed her saying, 'It's really good.' Fair enough, I thought and smiled back.

She moved like me and began to sweat like me. She even matched my pace and sweat poured out like drops of rain. *Wow*, I thought. *No kidding*. She didn't have long to go to get to the pinnacle. It took me two weeks to get a glimpse of what sweat looked like. I felt a tinge of jealousy I must confess, but c'est la vie. I minded my business until when I noticed her eyes rolled to the back of her head. Honestly, I thought she was in some sort of joy zone. *She must be some kind of gym wiz*. I found nothing out of the ordinary until she clutched at her chest and then began a slow descent. She was falling. She landed on the machine and slid down. She stopped moving. No sound came out of her mouth. In fact the only sound came from me. Short version of this story: after lots of water and fanning, she came to. Everyone gathered around her, deeply concerned. She made a promise to go see her physician before coming back. She nearly scared the living daylights out of everyone, but beyond that not much damage was done. We resumed our activity. I was so disturbed I cut my workout time short and left for home.

As I drove home I was reminded of one little fact, a clue as to what possibly went wrong. This lady hadn't been in the gym before or in a long time. She needed to start slowly. But most importantly, she didn't check with either her physician or gym instructor before using my settings. Those settings were meant for me.

As a result of the settings of my workout programme, I expect that, if I am consistent, I will get to my desired weight and fitness level.

If however someone else were to step on the same machine with my settings, it most probably would not work for them because it doesn't take their age and other details into account.

Yet, we often try to live our lives based on other people's settings. God doesn't have the same workout plans for all of us. His plans are specific and tailor-made for us.

He set a specific parameter for me and you to flourish and reach our full potential and He made NO OTHER plans to sustain us outside of these parameters.

We play dangerous games trying to work out on other people's turfs. We set ourselves up for failure when we leave our workout partner/trainer (God) and forage elsewhere. If we do this there's a likelihood that we would leave the gym (Life) with unfulfilled potential. We might even be scarred for life if we have unsavoury experiences. No matter how excited we are, we have to get our own specific instructions.

When you get to the gym of life, get on your own treadmill and sweat your own stuff. Whatever it is that God has called you specifically to do, step on it and start. Your personal trainer (God) awaits…

Ponder this:

Do you sometimes think your life runs haphazardly? There are specifics to our lives that God has carefully mapped out. God holds the blueprint. Get God. Get your specifics. Will you?

19. How Do You Brew?

Before the lightning strikes,
God is there.
Before the thunder roars,
God is there.
Before the enemy growls,
God is there.
God is there,
Watching
His champions win.

I was having a meltdown when these words barrelled into my spirit:
'What's your tea factor?'
'Huh?' I was taken aback.
'How do you brew?'
'Huh?' I repeated, confused.
'Deep, dark or light?'
'What!' I exclaimed.
'Aromatic and flavourful or just bland?'
'Lord,' I groaned, 'I'm having a meltdown and going through stuff and You initiate this kind of conversation?'
Silence.
I sat staring down into the tea swirling in the mug I cupped in my palms. My cup was half empty (pun intended). The steam had fizzled out.

It wasn't my favourite tea. It was a substitute that I had to get because I couldn't yet find 'the one' at the supermarket down the road. I had to make do. We are tea drinkers, albeit I the converted one. I married a tea drinker. We wake up to a nice steaming cup of Earl Grey (free advert for you Earl Grey) or Tetley's or PG Tips (and you too). And of course we favour loose tea as well.

There's an art to brewing this delicious drink. The hotter the water, the better the brew. These options make the difference: the temperature of the water, using teapot or flask, the mug or teacup, sugar or honey, creamer or milk or even plain with a splash or wedge of lemon. We do the whole works. You get any one of these ingredients wrong and you miss out on the authentic taste. Simple, yet you have to be a tea drinker to know the difference. The difference is the colour and the taste. The darker the tea, the better the brew and the more authentic the taste. Anything else is just hot milk.

My mind is whirling, twirling these questions around. I feel like I'm in a washing machine where all my thoughts are in a spin cycle, all jumbled up. It just doesn't make any sense. Yet I suspect that it's all to get the dirt out or fish the confusion out.

How can we go through life without any kind of pain, anguish or adversity? It's impossible. Don't I know that?

That tea bag sitting in its tin is of no use without the proverbial Hot Water. Pitch them side-by-side and all the tea bags look the same whatever the shape. The same white mesh with loose tea leaves inside. It's the 'hot water' that tells the tale each tea bag carries. It's the hot water that lets you know who its manufacturer is. Regardless of the packaging, if the quality is inferior, the 'hot water' will tell the secret. The hotter the water, the better the result.

We all look good on the surface. We have that 'churchy' smile, the happy family façade and all. Who wouldn't? We certainly don't want our dirty linen aired. No, we don't want people to know what stuff we're going through. We hope to keep it all together and just smile. Absolutely nothing wrong with that, but a time comes when that smile just won't crack open. It seems your face has been glued and you can't pull the smile muscles to work their magic. No, you're having a meltdown. I mean a really bad one that makes you wonder how you'll be able to pull through, if you do at all. How you do get over the pain and anguish that life enrolled you in?

The real question however is this: Do you have what it takes? Can you endure? Can you hang in there? Can you still stand? Well, we'll soon see when the 'hot water' trial comes. No matter how much faith you have, sometimes these trials come at your weakest moments, when you just don't have the strength to continue. It hits where it hurts the most. And you know what they say, when it rains, it typhoons.

Are you one of those who say 'Bring it on' when things go south? Really? Yeah! Me too. I'm seriously serious, cross my heart, BUT, notice the 'but' is in CAPS, there are times when I'm wondering when the barraging will stop. Times when I'm wondering when the Lord will pull the plug and stop the whirlpool before I drown; when I think I can't take it anymore and I just want to throw in the towel; when I think it's unfair. I mean, look at Mrs Tom and Mrs Harry down the road; they don't have issues. Yeah right! You think.

This is the 'hot water' stage. This is when the men are separated from the boys, oops, I mean when the babies are separated from the adults. This is when we know what you're really made of. Never mind the number of scriptures you can quote and how eloquent your prayers are. It's what's inside we're talking about, the hidden man of the heart. Who are you? Can you withstand the storm? Can you really? Hmmm.

Like the tea, we can't know what we're made of until we're dunked in hot water. Oh that 'hot water' will come. No exceptions. It's a given. We all go through adversity in varying degrees. That's life.

So when you're dropped in 'hot water' how do you brew? Ooze all your goodness and become aromatic and flavourful? Or do you just float and exude nothing, such that the water is discarded? It's not just that you're dunked in hot water; it's that that water needs to be extremely hot to get the best of the tea, or the best of you as the case may be.

You know that moment when you can finally understand 1% of how Jesus must have felt in the Garden of Gethsemane. Those groans of raw pain, pain so intense that even our Lord had to ask for the cup to pass, if not for a glorious future.

Note the versions of Proverbs 24:10 below, and the phrases in bold font. They sum things up neatly.

New International Version (NIV)

If you **falter in a time of trouble**, how small is your strength!

New Living Translation (NLT)

If you **fail under pressure**, your strength is too small.

New American Standard Version (NASV)

If you are **slack in the day of distress**, your strength is limited.

KJV

If thou **faint in the day of adversity**, thy strength is small.

The Message (MSG)

If you **fall to pieces in a crisis,** there wasn't much to you in the first place.

I just love the MSG version. Yes. If you're not secured and anchored in Christ, the storms of life will bulldoze you out of the way. What gives you staying power is God. Nothing else. Only God. You cannot withstand that hot water without having enough strength on the inside.

Now let's get to the good news. Take a look at Isaiah 40:29-31 and take note of the phrases in bold font.

29

He gives strength to the weary (NIV), energizes those who get tired (MSG), giveth power to the faint (KJV), and increases the power of the weak (NIV), gives fresh strength to dropouts (MSG), to them that have no might he increaseth strength (KJV).

30

Even youths grow tired and weary, and young men stumble and fall; but those who hope in the Lord will renew their strength (NIV), get fresh strength (MSG).

31

They will soar on wings like eagles (NIV); they will run and not grow weary (NIV), they won't lag behind (MSG), they shall not faint (KJV).

There's strength available. There are no guarantees that you will not face challenges. In fact, challenges are the hallmark of a Christian life. However, our triumph is guaranteed when we trust Him. When the hot water comes, brew dark and strong. Let your aroma fill the room and let your flavour be pleasant. Brew dark and strong. That's your strength.

Ponder this:

Are you having a challenging time right now? Does it seem like God is so far away? Let me assure you that God is closer than even the breath you breathe. He will strengthen you and walk with you out of the valley. Trust Him.

20. Turn The Other Cheek and Still Be Happy

Twas a shameful thing
That happened on the Cross
Where thieves and robbers dine
My Saviour crucified.
Left all His glory behind
To bear my shame and pain
How dare they slap my master?
How dare they beat him up?
He chose to turn the other cheek
That we may win this war.

That man didn't just ruffle your feathers, he trampled all over them, spat on them and dragged them all over the floor until they tore in pieces. What do you do? Do you give him your second most delicate wing since the Bible said to turn the other cheek? Or do you slap him upside down? Give him a piece of your mind and kick foolhardiness out of him? How dare he? How dare he cross you?

I personally believe this is an area that requires a great deal of restraint and wisdom. When the Bible says turn the other cheek, what does it mean? Does it mean you let people walk all over you? Drag you around like a rag doll and manipulate you like a puppet?

First and foremost, I believe we are meant to be peacemakers.

I believe the scriptures expect us to pursue peace at all times. That's why we are called 'Children of God', because we're meant to be peacemakers (Matthew 5:9). Pursuing peace is an active phrase. When faced with a difficult situation or person we are expected to negotiate peace first, yet not at any cost. What do I mean? Find the peaceful slant in any situation. You can only control your feelings and actions. You can't control those of others. Your peaceful stance is meant to douse every tension from the other side.

However, in the event that doesn't seem to work, stand on the truth. If you need to apologise for a wrongdoing, by all means do that and then stand on the right principle. You are better off erring on the side of caution than being presumptuous.

Be ready to negotiate for the sake of peace, but don't sell your soul as a result.

Secondly, find God's specific wisdom in the given situation. Peace is the umpire for knowing the will of God. So you're already on the right path pursuing peace. Now do a search of events. Be a little analytical. Have you erred? Swallow that humble pie and do the needful. You've been misunderstood? Happens. State your case without sounding too defensive. Now that you've done all you know to do, stand still. Don't grovel. That's not turning the other cheek.

Pursuing peace is turning the other cheek.

Turning the other cheek doesn't mean you lay down like a doormat and let people walk back and forth, dragging mud all over you. Absolutely not!

People will hurt and upset you every day. That's a given and there's nothing you can do about it. Actually, there is something you can do about it. You can choose to get riled up and camp on the issue and put a placard up so the world can see what others have done to you or you can move on. You can choose to fight back because you don't want anyone messing with you, or you can forgive and stay in the same place where you first got hurt. Those are two extremes by the way.

Also, you can quickly forgive, yet wise up and move out of harm's way. You certainly don't want to be steamrolled again. You can give people the benefit of the doubt just so you don't jump too quickly to conclusions and hold grudges. You can choose to let go, leave things in God's hands and let Him resolve it. It's the wise thing to do to try to make peace where possible. Always choose to make peace first. You can be angry and yet not sin.

Now if the pursuant refuses to be at peace, you can simply shake the dust off of your feet, smile and be happy. You have successfully turned the other cheek and guess what? You're still happy. Why? Because you pursued peace wisely as God has commanded. Whether is it received or not is no longer your headache. Always make sure you have ticked your boxes.

Now be happy!

Ponder this:

Do you find it difficult to control your indignation when people offend you? Guess what? Offense will always come. We are human. Do you know God can give you the wisdom at every point in time to deal with offense, such that you're not under its hold? You're bigger than that. You can deal with these situations and be happy. Choose happy.

THE PAUSE

A time to rend, and a time to sew; a time to keep *silence*, and a time to speak; Ecclesiastic 3:7 (KJV)

1. God Broke My Heart

The book, ***When God Breaks Your Heart*** by Ed Underwood, inspired this chapter. I have been instructed to write, to tell everyone that at some point in my life God broke my heart. Yes. Surprised?

I was so expectant. So how then can I explain the delays? How does it work? I've prayed, fasted, declared and just about done everything according to the books. Why are the lines not falling in pleasant places?

Despite the wait, God broke my heart.

It wasn't quite what I expected. Failing to see that it's not that the prayer and fasting didn't work. It's that God's love for me is deeper than my comprehension, and death as we know it is not the cessation of existence, but a transition to eternity. I depended more on my faith, my eloquence, and my prayers, and chose to turn a deaf ear to God's sovereignty. I didn't want to surrender lest I hear something I wasn't quite ready to accept. I thought God broke my heart when He said 'NO', because I didn't let Him lift me up to where He is, to view things from the top. I wanted to embrace only the finite and disregard the infinite. I wanted the intrinsic rather than the divine. I wanted normal rather than super-normal. I forgot the exploits of faith. I forgot to view things from eternity's perspective. I forgot to trust in God's love. I forgot to trust at all.

Instead I chose to grieve which is why:

I sit on the pew in church like a spectator completely numb and oblivious to all. I feel nothing. Neither the praise nor the worship moves me. A battle is raging and I'm not willing it to stop. The churning going on inside fuels my angst. An emotion I had failed to acknowledge until now. What was it they said about the many stages of grief? Was it shock first or anger? Was it anguish or denial? It really doesn't matter. I feel it all rolled up in one, each jostling for space in my mind.I am losing it and don't recognize the downward spiral to which these hideous emotions are plunging me.

I am grieving. That is a sad fact. I failed to write. I failed to be coherent. I failed to let myself grieve. Instead, I stare at the world that seems to be meaningless now. It has become a stage where we all step up to act, to wear masks and be who we are not. We weep, we laugh, and we live a life that doesn't belong to us. A borrowed life as Paul rightly said. So why do we fight as though beating the air? What's the big deal about life anyway?

I am grieving and it feels so surreal. Like life is lived only in my dreams. I have nothing tangible to touch but dreams and memories. Catching up with reality gets daunting. I fear to forget voices, love and laughter. They often say time heals, but I believe God heals better. I laugh inside at my own affirmation. I haven't believed God for a while. I have been in a vortex of confusion. My body is still in touch with reality, but the rest of me, well; I am clueless as to where they are. Disconnected and disjointed. Yes, of course, I love God, I believe in Him and I trust Him wholeheartedly, yet I feel completely disconnected from Him. I know all things work together for our good, yet I feel helpless in this case. I know God loves me with a perfect love, have experienced it countless times and have shared with others, yet I feel disjointed. My body and emotions are not on talking terms. My mind? Lord, have mercy! It's like a jigsaw puzzle, a million pieces of it scattered all over a grassy field.

I am grieving. I feel like I'm waltzing to a joy and sadness funk. I want life lived my way with time within my grasp. But that is absurd. There is this gasping for breath, gasping to wake up from this dream. I am supposed to wake up and move on, right? But I'm hurting and I need to heal. I have read many stories of those who hold their own even as they grieve; yet I'm falling apart. I am raw from pain and I cannot follow a system or precept or design for getting over grief. I have been told to wrap it up, cry, scream and make it short. I wish I could shed gallons of tears. I cannot. I cry, but find it pointless, as it doesn't completely relieve me. Odd, but that's me.

Look at me. I'm gushing with pain. I selfishly wish to share my pain with the world. I cannot bottle it alone inside. Implosion is not a good word.

So I sit in church from service to service, numb through and through and untouched. No, my heart is not hardened. I think not, at least. I am just not sure if the tears I cry — if and when they do come — will be mild or wild. Something died in me when I thought I lost the centre of my being. It was hope. I hoped for so long until I pushed hope to arm's length. I was so cocksure I prayed powerfully enough. I pushed God's sovereignty to my blind spot. So this loss of hope rattled the foundation of my faith because I believed in my own prayers more than I believed in God's sovereignty over all things.

Though my mind was the first to accept reality, it never really placed things in a neat pile. It more or less pushed everything to the subconscious to deal with. And my subconscious pushed it back out and my body got the brunt of it. It reacted wildly and something snapped when the doctor said to me, 'Don't lose your mind.' I think I was on the verge of losing my mind. I had crossed the line. I acted like everything was okay and I was fine and living with reality. Truth be told, I was far from reality.

Although I crumbled on the inside, I finally let go. I couldn't pray nor muster the strength. I whispered 'help' not trusting that my own strength could carry me through or far. And then God whispered back 'Peace! Let it go.' I know enough to understand that God did the best for me despite my initial doubts. Now to the business of healing or dealing with this pain the right way. I finally realize that there are two in this journey, God and me. I only need to whisper 'help' and He'd come to my rescue like He'd done in the past and He will do again and again. That the answer didn't come like I hoped doesn't negate God's love for me, and that God responds even to my whisper is more than enough for me.

I questioned God.

As always, I want to reason things out with God. I want to question Him, His motives and plans; after all I'm thrown in the mix. I should have a say, shouldn't I?

I questioned God's timings and seasons. Like Israel, I longed for garlic and onions instead of manna; forgetting for a moment the years of slavery and servitude. How soon we forget these things huh? People's issues remain outstanding prayer points and years go by without any answer from heaven. And I was so filled with confusion and so torn inside I threw questions at God.

As I waited for answers to my questions — more like grumblings and accusations, and I'm being totally honest here — I listened to a message that spoke directly to my heart.

This preacher expounded the issue of timing and God's sovereignty. Some things we have control over, but most things we do not. We must give room for God's sovereignty, which can sometimes override our belief system. As if that wasn't enough, my pastor's message, just the other day, centred on timing, seasons and God's sovereignty. I tell you, I sank in my seat. Yep, God was hounding me. I avoided my pastor's eyes as much as I could and chided myself for sitting in one of the front rows. That message was a missile headed for me.

As I thumbed through the scriptures, God spoke to my heart and instructed me to turn to the book of Job. Uh-oh. I knew I was in trouble. He told me to read chapters 38 through to 40. Pause, dog-ear this page or bookmark it. Go read it all and come back. Share in my admonition. Ha ha!

As soon as I opened the chapter, His voice boomed in my spirit: Where were you?

"What!' I looked about me.

His question jolted and stilled me at the same time. All the time my pastor was preaching, I was in the examination room with God. I was rooted to my seat. Who would I turn to, to bail me out?

Oh no, He didn't let me off:

2 "Who is this who darkens counsel
By words without knowledge?
3 Now prepare yourself like a man;
I will question you, and you shall answer Me.

4 "WHERE WERE YOU WHEN I LAID THE
FOUNDATIONS OF THE EARTH?
Tell Me, if you have understanding.
5 Who determined its measurements?
Surely you know!

Or who stretched the line upon it?
6 To what were its foundations fastened?"

Please help me out here. Were you there too, at the foundation of the world? I wasn't. I hadn't the foggiest notion what happened and when. I haven't the foggiest notion even now where tomorrow is and my place in it. Yet, I dared to question. I broke down in my seat. Just then, pastor called for worship, and the music and instruments drowned out my wailings; what perfect timing. Oh boy, I wailed like a baby.

God is sovereign and though He lets us have our way sometimes, it must frustrate Him when we question His plans for us.

I remember watching a video with my daughter a while ago of our world and the solar system. In comparison with the largest known star in the universe, VY Canis Majoris, our earth is like a tiny dot that it will take over a thousand years for it to circle on the fastest jet plane around this star once. As big as that star is, it is only a tiny dot amongst several hundred billion stars forming our galaxies and there are a hundred billion galaxies out there. This should make us reflect on the greatness of our God.

If He can create such vast and complex galaxies and yet create tiny you and me on a tiny planet and still call us His own, what exactly am I questioning? His greatness, His wisdom, His power and majesty, or His capacity to love me to infinity and beyond? What exactly am I questioning? That He made a promise and it hasn't yet come to pass, or whether He is capable of fulfilling His promise? That He permitted the loss of a loved one? What exactly am I questioning? That He is God all by Himself and there is none other?

Deepest sigh.

Selah!

PARABLES

I will open my mouth in a *parable*: I will utter
dark sayings of old: Psalm 78:2(KJV)

All these things spake Jesus unto the multitude
in *parables*; and without a parable spake he
not unto them: Matthew 13:34 (KJV)

1. The Boxing Ring

When God sits and laughs,
The foundations of the world will rattle.
When God breathes out loud,
The ocean beds are uncovered.
When God fights for you,
Selah should be your next word.

Have you ever been inside a boxing ring about to fight? You're whatever weight title and you're the recipient of some hard knocks and slugging by a heavy weight champion. Not a pretty sight I can assure you: the ugly bruises, the broken tooth hanging, the swollen eyelids, the shifted jaw and all the tell-tale signs that you've been through hell and back. The money better be worth it, would be your next thought. At least you can be fixed up. It's all about the money anyway. That's why you're in that pathetic ring, being booed or cheered by the pathetic crowd for pathetic reasons like fame and fortune. That's the bottom line, my friend.

Now I know of a heavy weight champion who has never ever lost a fight and you don't want to mess with Him. Never! Don't even consider it in your mind. However, thoughtless fobs do try and mess with Him. If they had any brains at least they would fight in an open field where if they lost they could take off on their heels. Instead, they choose a boxing ring with an audience round about. They hedge themselves in and strut all around in flamboyant attires hoping to be buoyed by the cheers of the audience. What do you think will happen when the heavy weight champion eventually comes in?

Abraham, the father of the left hook

Abraham can tell you what. He's in the audience yet not part of the audience. He's not the manager, for the heavy weight champion doesn't need a manager. He's the son of the heavy weight champion. He's seated to watch a fight being fought on his behalf. Let him tell you his story.

In Genesis 12:10-20, God handpicked Abram and cut a covenant with him. God's plan was for Abram to be invincible until he had lived and fulfilled his destiny. God's plan included giving him a son to carry on his legacy and the covenant relationship established with God. However at the moment, Abram was childless. Beyond children, God planned to make Abram big enough to be reckoned with ages after his death. Abram was going to be larger than life. He was not just going to be rich and famous, plus the invincible part; he was going to be the conduit pipe through which people the world over would know about God. He was the picture perfect servant of God.

Abram wanted a child, but God was more invested in giving him a child, much more than he reckoned or even realized. God didn't plan to just bless Abram. He wanted the blessing to be the automatic inheritance of his descendants. Abram set about the task of keeping his part of the covenant with God. He was to serve God with all of his being and serve no other. That was it. The promised child would come through the only woman God recognized as his wife, Sarai. She was to be the mother of the promised child.

A few years down the road, famine drove Abram down to Egypt. In Egypt Abram became exposed. This was a land that didn't worship the same God as he did. This was a land whose ruler's word was the law. Yet his sojourn in Egypt meant he needed protection if need be. He had been given the task of protecting Sarai to ensure no harm came to her so that she was in good health and well enough to carry and birth the promised child. As a husband and future father, that was his job. Yet as they approached

Egypt, he had inkling what could transpire. He probably heard of the fame of Pharoah and his love for women, foreign and all.

Abram bargained with his wife to pretend she was his sister. In a sense she was, but in the truer sense she was his wife. His fear for his own life led him to scheme like this. If only he fully understood the covenant he cut with God. God was bound to cover His own end of the covenant. All His promises hadn't yet been fulfilled so how in the world was Abram going to lose his life before God fulfilled His promise? Not possible. God always honours His word. His reputation is tied up with His word, His promises, and His proclamations. He could never go back on His word because that was the basis of His integrity. Abram forgot that the promised child was yet to be born. He bargained out of fear.

Sarai was so beautiful all of Egypt noticed, to the point Pharoah just had to have her in his vicinity. She was that breath taking. Then began the outpouring of favour towards Abram because of Sarai. I believe it was all a well-conceived plan by God because that was when Abram began to amass additional wealth; sheep, oxen, assess, camels and slaves. They were just giving Abram stuff while Abram thought he was trying to protect his own life. If only he understood that the covenant child had to come through him and Sarai, and not through him alone.

Perhaps Pharoah had started courting Sarai. Perhaps he began to make plans to both woo and add her to his harem. Perhaps he was plagued by lustful thoughts and just had to have her at all cost. Perhaps he had started the process of fully acquiring her. All the pomp and pageantry, the ceremonies and all had been set up. Sarai was being bathed in aromatic oils and immersed in other marital rituals. Obviously, Abram couldn't protect her from Pharaoh any more. Abram had abandoned her to her own fate. Who was going to fight for her, for them? Who was going to ensure the promised children came?

When God had had enough, He plagued Pharaoh's household. It was the type of plague they'd never seen before. It just pointed them to Abram. They knew it had to be because of Abram. It had never happened until Sarai entered the palace. God came on the scene to fight for Abram's covenant. Abram had a part to play and while through fear he almost jeopardized the terms of the covenant, God came quickly to the rescue. God fought for Abram and Sarai to protect and preserve not just their lives and union but His promise to them.

God dealt such a huge blow to Pharoah, gave him such a TKO that he had to let Abram and his household leave. God was more passionate about His covenant with Abraham than even Abraham himself.

"My covenant will I not break, nor alter the thing that is gone out of my lips." Psalm89:34.

We have a covenant with the almighty God, our father and He is has respect for His words. He would do whatever it takes to ensure the covenant is not jeopardised. His covenant with us is precious to Him.

Ponder this:

Do you know God is in your corner? He fights for you. He has never lost a battle and yours won't be the first. Brag on God! You win all the time.

2. Don't Mess With My Quarterback

We live life
Together,
We fight battles
Together,
We share joys
Together,
We share pain
Together,
We stay strong
Together,
When we are
Together.

Outside of athletics, I know zilch about sports, and least of all American football, which I gather, is much different from soccer (which most of the world calls football). On one of those weekends I found myself watching the movie, *The Game Plan*. I have this habit of watching movies beyond the intention of mere entertainment. I question the plot and I'm always curious about what's not being said or told, what could have been, should have been and a slew of other commentaries. In this case, here's what hooked me: the lead actor happens to be a quarterback player who was injured because someone from the rival team tackled him badly. He was knocked out cold and couldn't play for that season. Even though he wasn't fully recovered, he couldn't bare to watch his team lose over and over again. He decided to get back on the field and help his team members even if he had to hobble on the field. You see, you have to understand how it works and how crucial the role of the quarterback is.

Quarterbacks are members of the offensive team and line up directly behind the offensive line. Quarterbacks are the leaders of the offensive team, responsible for calling the play in the huddle. The quarterback role is one of the most visible and important roles on the team. The quarterback touches the ball on nearly every offensive play and has a great deal of responsibility both in calling plays and making decisions during the play. Most quarterbacks are on the field for every offensive play leaving only for injury or when the game's outcome is no longer in doubt.

This quarterback hobbled and limped his way back into the game and what do you know, the hefty looking dude from the other team tackled him again. What's a semi-recovered man to do? His team members rallied round and blocked every avenue of flying limbs aimed at the injured man to prevent further injury. They rammed muscle into every opposing team member, sped down the field at lightning speed, wielding in and out, guarding jealously their quarterback to ensure the ball stayed safe and he made the home run.

Suddenly, out of nowhere, the opposing six-pack dude showed up again, ramming his full weight into our quarterback but his mate was close by and he shoved his full weight back on this opponent and sent him flying while their quarterback made the safe home run. Then this teammate went back and spat out at the baddie, 'Don't mess with my quarterback.' The long and short of it was that they won not just because their quarterback was back in the game and that he was good, but because they covered him at every angle where they should. That is what a team does: even when the quarterback is the main man, the front-line man, the team must still work together and watch each other's backs.

God's plan for man was for him to be in company, never alone; whether parents, spouse, children, friends or neighbours. In every group, every team, every gathering, there's a quarterback. There's someone who represents and speaks for the group or plays a significant role. And sometimes, there are quarterbacks in our personal lives too, people God places strategically in our lives to speak into our lives, take the flack for us, give to us, and make life worth much more. In other words, add value.

I have met such people who have taken the role of quarterbacks in my life. They have challenged adversity, faced issues head-on, soothed a wound, wiped a tear, or simply made me laugh through their rich words of encouragement. And in the same vein, I have shared their traumas, joys, bad tackles and pain. We all know the enemy of our soul, the one who hates who we are and whose we are.

Suppose you understand this as I hope that you would. There's a team and you're on it. You play a significant role and so does everyone, but your quarterback on this team is your pastor. He's the one who makes the home run and causes your team to win. You do understand however that he cannot make that home run just by being the quarterback? It doesn't matter the size of his muscles or experience; without you and the rest of the team, he can do absolutely diddlysquat. He can run all he likes with the ball safely clutched in his arm. If the opposing team makes a dash for him, he's a goner without you and the rest of the team. They're going to crush him and it will take a miracle to get him out from that pile of human beings alive.

Do you leave your quarterback on the field to be pummelled to death? Remember he brings you the home run. No, you don't leave him. You support him. You defend him. You speak for him. Don't let them mess with your quarterback.

Your quarterbacks could be your spouse, your children, your pastor, your boss, and even your staff. We've got to have each other's backs. There's strength in unity. We wield more power when we huddle together to fight a common enemy.

Remember what the scripture says:

'Again I say unto you, That if two of you shall agree on earth as touching any thing that they shall ask, it shall be done for them of my Father which is in heaven.' — (Matthew 18:19, KJV)

Or the verse that says:

'A person standing alone can be attacked and defeated, but two

can stand back-to-back and conquer. Three are even better, for a triple-braided cord is not easily broken.' — (Ecclesiastes 4:12, NLT)

We win when we work together. We win when we have each other's backs. We win when we're in harmony. Just like a broom; you can break a broomstick easily, but you cannot break a broom no matter how hard you try. It's not always about who shines the most. It's about winning together.

When Christ said He was coming for a church, He was referring to a body, a group or team of people, not just one individual. In God's kingdom, there's no lone ranger. Our roles are different and rightly so because we need to function differently, but in our difference we are meant to fit into a completed puzzle.

It is tempting to want to fly the solo kite but guess what? You get better returns investing in and living with others.

Ponder this:

Do you remember God saying 'Let us make man like Us' in Genesis 1? That's God demonstrating unity and togetherness. He wants us to work together.

3. Ozymandias

Though we achieve greatness,
Though our names are carved in stone,
Though we perform monumental feats,
And deem we would always
Matter through the years,
Except the Lord builds the house,
Everything will crumble,
Ravaged by time and mortality.

God has a sense of humour, the best ever. I say this because time is immaterial to Him and while we are in a tug-of-war with it, He gently nudges us along His plans. When we follow God's plans for our lives, time begins to make sense. Before then, it's just an anthology of numbers.

This is the story of Ozymandias, a king who ruled long ago and forgot he didn't hold tomorrow in his hands. Read for yourself and see where his follies lay.

I met a traveller from an antique land
Who said: "Two vast and trunkless legs of stone
Stand in the desert. Near them on the sand,
Half sunk, a shattered visage lies, whose frown
And wrinkled lip and sneer of cold command
Tell that its sculptor well those passions read

Which yet survive, stamped on these lifeless things,
The hand that mocked them and the heart that fed.
And on the pedestal these words appear:
'My name is Ozymandias, King of Kings:
Look on my works, ye mighty, and despair!'
Nothing beside remains. Round the decay
Of that colossal wreck, boundless and bare,
The lone and level sands stretch far away.

By Percy B Shelley (1818)

Ozymandias built an empire, with monuments and legacy meant to last forever. But then, he predicted wrong. He didn't live forever and none of his monuments or buildings survived the desolation of time. All that remained were pieces of his statue: his stone head with his formidable scowl, some legs partially buried in the sand, and inscriptions that describe his 'mighty works'. He belittled his mortality; a mere man who was revered far and wide. He assumed godhood and called himself the king of kings, a title reserved for non other than Jesus Christ our Lord and Saviour. And God had the last laugh.

For centuries, men have always wanted to rule men. Of all the things God permitted man to partake of, His clear instruction had been that man would have dominion over His creation but not over another man. The greatest desire of man has always been power and dominion, not just over God's creation, but also over other men; to be like God and wield unlimited power and be worshipped by men. This thirst for power has driven conquerors and leaders of all ages. From Nimrod to Ottoman, to Alexander the Great, to Caesar, to Hitler and present-day leaders, man's greatest thirst has been to control this unique creature made in the exact image and likeness of God.

We have seen kingdoms come and go and it's the same story: serve us or die. Wars through the ages were born from the tiny embers of lust for power and dominion. The same thirst that the devil introduced in the Garden of Eden, telling Eve and Adam that if they ate of the tree of Knowledge of Good and Evil they would be as gods, knowing all things as God and therefore be in control. What he in effect introduced was the thirst for the wrong kind of control because already Adam and Eve had been given a mandate to dominate. With all the things in the garden that Adam and Eve had to tend to, they were still lured to seek something else, something outside of their familiar territory, something that promised greatness. The devil still plays the same game today. He lures men to seek to dominate over one another for greatness; but no man can truly be great without God.

Outside of the gigantic feats resulting in massive destruction committed by these leaders, we still have regular fellows who seek to exert some form of control or the other over men perceived to be weaker. The tools they have used include money, race, class or social status, education and physical looks. If you're nothing like me then I'm better than you therefore you need to hold me in higher esteem. The history of the world is riddled with men enslaving men, wars and power drunkenness, but we need not go into that. What we need to closely monitor is the subtle evil in the regular society; the evil of domination, intimidation and eventual manipulation—all manifestations of control.

The enemy seeks to control our lives so that we live in rebellion to God. He wishes to make us slaves to his whims so that we oppose God, question God and ultimately rebel. The evils of society stem from the unnatural desire to control man or time in which case, the former is unethical and the latter impossible.

I have since discovered that leadership is a far cry from control. Leaders serve, inspire, encourage and motivate. Control freaks use people for things. Power is intoxicating and can cause major devastation when it's not controlled.

I bet many kingdoms and people feared Ozymandias in his time of reign. He must have been revered, albeit reluctantly. He would have been a mighty warrior, conquering lands and cities, taking people as slaves and basking in riches and wealth. He was like a god; and why not? He had control. Until the day the Almighty controller Himself took away two things Ozymandias had no control over; time and life.

Not only did Ozymandias' time stop ticking, his life, kingdom and monuments became relics that disintegrated into sands of time. He is no longer the ruler to be feared or remembered. He could no longer be called the king of kings because he couldn't control mortality.

But have you heard about the King who never dies, who rules and reigns from eternity to eternity; the King who is not buried and forgotten in the sands of time? The King who holds the title today and forever? His name is Jesus.

Only God holds the title of the 'Almighty'. No mortal can claim that. And so while men like to play god and act like they will live forever out of their own will, God is laughing. What an utter waste of time!

Live your life for God while you still have the breath in you, for soon your time will be up and the life that you live will be judged in eternity, not here. If you have to build monuments, make sure they have to do with lives. Don't build monuments to ensure you outlast everyone and live forever. Build with eternity in mind. And by the way, we are not meant to use people for our satisfaction; we are meant to love and live with them, and conquer together.

Ponder this:

The simple truth is this: when we yield full control of our lives to God, we also forfeit the right to control other people. We are meant to lead, not control. Can I get an 'Amen' people?

4. Fresh from the Source

Just as Jesus aims
For your heart
Where the source
Of your life flows,
Aim for the source
Where the essence
Of your life
Will flow:
God's heart
The source of life.

I've been to Dubai only a few times and on each trip, I have always got a visa locally until I discovered another way to pay for a visa directly from Dubai. On arrival at Dubai during a recent trip, I found out that the Dubai source was way cheaper than my local contact. From then on I started paying far less than I normally would. Until I got an inside source, I probably would have kept paying premium.

The source is where I get the original, the authentic. The closer you are to the source the more authentic what you get is. Sometimes, the word of God gets watered down whilst it's being ministered to us. Open to interpretation and misinterpretation. Even the most anointed message is at best open to misinterpretation because it is still through a human vessel we hear it and we also as vessels may have the issue of hearing correctly. The word of God in its pure state is infallible, full of power and authority.

What makes the word of God rich and authentic and real is when, after having heard the message, we go back to the word and start to do our own independent search of what is true after which we prayerfully work it out in our lives. We have to be actively engaged and be intimate with the word of God. Until we connect with the source, most times we could be short changed.

The Bible says we know in part and we prophesy in part. There are both ministry gifts and gifts of the Holy Spirit. Not one church, denomination or minister has the anointing nor exclusive knowledge of all parts of the Bible. God gifts different people differently. The Bible is the only source of all sides and all truths. Some may specialise in healing because that's their area of revelation whilst some may be specialist in leadership or wisdom or prophecy.

When we connect with the source we not only get to understand our own unique area of calling and assignment, we also understand as much of the whole that God wants us to understand.

It's dangerous to only listen to messages by men of God and never read, study or search the scriptures ourselves. There's a place for the church and our pastor's messages and blessings, but our personal relationship with God must never be compromised.

There's something powerful in chewing the word of God and skilfully applying it directly to your own situation. That's growth and that's when we begin to operate in *sonship*, not as babies still feeding on the milk of the word. God wants us all to get to that level. That's why it's vital to always stay focused on the source and not so much on the vessel to the detriment of our salvation. It's your direct connection to the source that sustains you. Every other connection works quite all right, but was never intended to be the anchor or the foundation to build on. That's why going to church without a relationship with God will simply make you religious, not a connected, spirit-filled child of God.

There are a great many benefits in being connected to the source.

You get the undiluted truth.

Like fresh water from a mountain source, you get purity.

You get freshness. Freshness revives and breathes life into you. Life means health. Health means strength. Strength means longevity and stability. All that means a healthy and stable Christian life.

So which source are you drawing breath from? What is your life source? Who or what sustains you at moments of crisis? What is your anchor? You see, I have since discovered that no matter how much people help us during crisis (and believe me we need it) there must also be strength lodged deep inside of us that we can draw from during those times when people have to live their lives and move on with it. That strength gets lodged inside when we commune with God and dig deep into His words. One of the scriptures that keeps me going especially during a crisis:

'For I know the plans I have for you,' says the LORD. 'They are plans for good and not for disaster, to give you a future and a hope.' (Jeremiah 29:11, NLT)

Ponder this:

Do you know God for yourself or do you only depend on your Pastor? Good as it may be, you need your own connection. God doesn't have grandchildren. He has children. God is easy to get to know. He's waiting for you.

5. Contain The Fire

Is there fire in your bones?
Control it, lest it burn you too.
Is there fire in your words?
Control it lest it starts a war.
Is there power in your grasp?
Control it, lest it destroys even you.

A spread of colourful sports and fitness attire filled the hall. Air conditioners hummed, blasting cool air that didn't seem to make any difference. Shouts, rants, raves, grunts and heaves rend the air in sync with the music pumping from the speakers.

They pumped their legs, kicked, lifted weights and moved to the beats along with the fitness instructor, matching every move jump-by-jump, skip-by-skip. Sweat poured like drops of rain, as the mixed look of delight and exhaustion electrified the atmosphere. They were on a mission.

Then he strolled in, flexing his chest, biceps bulging and head snapping to the left and right as if he was about to face a challenge headlong. He swept his gaze around the hall, observed the women hooping about and the left side of his lips upturned in a sneer. No doubt this was child's play compared to his usual weights and endurance exercises. However, he needed his abs done as well as to build more stamina.

After the timeout whistle went off, he took his place behind the women, cracking his knuckles and stretching his neck, ready for the next twenty minutes of aerobics. He couldn't wait to tick this off as done so he could quickly get back to his weight training.

After a short break, the music started. The instructor took a leap in the air and the women followed in tow. He suddenly found he couldn't lift off. He was earthbound and no matter how much strength he mustered, and he had plenty of it, he just couldn't lift off the ground the way the women did, landing almost like cats. They took off again, limbs going in different directions.

He tried to match up to the moves, but he had too much muscle in the way restricting the fluid movement he observed with the women. He needed to get a grip on himself. These women were weaker than him and were no match for his bulging muscles. What was wrong with him? He tried yet again, straining and reaching out to duplicate every move, but he bungled it each time. He checked himself in the floor to ceiling mirror, watching his own moves, and almost gagged. His body wasn't cooperating and he just wasn't able to copy any of the moves without looking ridiculous.

He certainly didn't want to make a fool of himself and let these women get the better of him. He made one last ditch attempt to strain his poor limbs to comply and jump nimbly as they should, and ended up on the floor howling in pain. He had torn a ligament and lay spread-eagle on the floor. Oh the shame!

The music stopped and the women rushed to his side.

'Ah, so sorry.'

'Are you okay?'

Of course he wasn't okay. Never mind his muscles, his ego was flat out punctured and deflated. Oh the shame!

Make that double shame; the women helped him up, each grabbing onto taut muscles and hoisting him to a sitting position.

He wondered what went wrong.

What went wrong was that he controlled his movement wrong. He applied strength and pressure rather than patience, skill and coordination. The women he thought were weak had learned to harness and control their limbs to create fluid movements without causing any injury. It takes weeks and months of continuous practice to get to that stage. The more correct control you apply, the easier it is to get the desired result.

Power and control when used wrongly or by the unskilled often have devastating consequences. Power should not be given to the untrained. When we exert power wrongly, we hurt people, including ourselves in the long run. No matter how much we think we fit the bill, to have access to power is a privilege we should never take for granted. When power is used for the good of all, people rejoice.

Jesus had access to power. That's why He healed the sick and performed many miracles for the benefit of others. Power should not be to solely benefit oneself. That's abuse of power.

True power and authority is really not about arrogance, charm, charisma or striking good looks even if that's what the world yells for. It's about character, humility, wisdom and proven skill.

What did David, the man after God's heart, do when he had the opportunity to kill Saul (1 Samuel 24)? He didn't take matters in his own hands simply because he had the power to exact revenge. Actually, it takes a lot more strength to exercise control and restraint than to fling power out there.

One of the parts of Jesus' time on earth I've found the most fascinating was when He and the disciples had to cross over to the other side after a long period of preaching and teaching (Mark 4:35-41). There was a storm. When He arose from deep sleep, in a very calm voice, He spoke to the stormy sea: 'Peace, be still!' The winds ceased immediately. Now that's what I call power.

When people have power it changes how they act and behave. True power is often synonymous with calmness, wisdom. Have you noticed? You have such power that you don't feel the need to try and prove it or ram it down anyone's throat. Any other use of power whether spiritual, physical or secular is demonic and totally wrong.

Do you know that as a child of God you have tremendous power available to you? Try the name of Jesus out for size. Every knee under the heavens and the earth bow to that name, and that's the name you carry. Try the blood of Jesus and every negative influence is rendered useless. Now use that same power like Jesus did, to save and to deliver.

Ponder this:

Did you know? Your mere whisper of Jesus' name carries tremendous power. Use it and rattle the gates of hell.

6. Shout

Shout to yourself
That you made it.
Shout to send tremors
To the depths of hell.
Shout for joy,
Shout for victory,
When all is said and done.

I honestly don't believe I have to shout when I pray, for God to hear me. Do you? As the title of this book suggests, even your mere whisper is audible enough for God to catch.

Of course there's a place for shouting, but to believe until I 'prayerfully' shout 'to' God He won't hear me, is a fallacy in my humble opinion. I'm at my comfort level when I pray in my normal voice. I get distracted when I shout or try to shout and I lose my train of thought or the reason why I'm shouting in the first place. I'd like to pray and hear God speak as and while I'm praying, like a two-way communication thing. It doesn't work for me when I shout and I don't stop to hear God. I hardly hear myself much less the voice of God. I don't just want to throw loud words at God and then walk away expecting God to answer the prayer. Now with these seeming limitations does that mean if I pray without shouting, God won't hear me? I repeat, I think not. I know some people feel energized and ready to conquer when they shout, but it shouldn't replace a deep-seated conviction of what we're praying for, and from what standpoint; that of a finished victory simply being reinforced by us.

When I attend prayer meetings where the prayer leader says something like, 'Shout' and 'Pray' in the same context as though they can be interchangeable, I usually get in a garbled mess. I know it probably works for a lot of people, but for me, shouting doesn't enhance my prayers. Nor does it necessarily engender boldness or fervency. It is not even universal, as I see that we Africans like to shout.

We may begin to cite **James 5:16b (KJV), 'The effectual fervent prayer of a righteous man availeth much.'** Let me assure you that you don't necessarily need to shout to be effective or fervent.

I checked the dictionary for synonyms of the word effectual or effective. Here's a list, though not exhaustive: powerful, authoritative, successful, efficient, able, prevailing, potent, commanding. It's not in the multitude of words or the pitch or tempo of your voice. It's the authority behind it. Jesus commanded respect both on earth and in hell because of the authority behind His words.

For the word fervent I found: passionate, obsessive, fiery, zealous, and enthusiastic.

Let's look at our scripture verse above from two other translations.

'The prayer of a righteous person is powerful and effective.' (NIV) In other words, shout all you like, if you live a messed up, unholy life, God is not gonna hear you. Period!

'The earnest (heartfelt, continued) prayer of a righteous man makes tremendous power available [dynamic in its working].' (AMP). Is there a connection with God? Is your heart really in the prayer or are you just marking time and 'fulfilling all righteousness'?

For prayer to produce result:

1. We must first be righteous (By reason of our relationship with God. Forgiven; standing right with God.)

2. The words we pray must have inherent power or be backed by authority. That means we must pray the word of God. (Hebrews

4:12) When applied to any given situation, it is quick and power-ful enough to dismantle every stronghold. The word of God itself has power. It doesn't need an addendum. Another reason why ad-dendums are unnecessary, so we don't fall into error.

3. We must be persistent (The unjust judge, Luke 18:1-8) We must mean business. We must be determined to pray until we see evi-dent results; coming back again and again on the same issue until we see the result we desire.

In order not to short-change myself with mere lexicons, I decided also to do a quick study on the word 'shout' and instances when the people of God engaged in a 'shout' or why it was used in the Bible. Here's what I discovered from the listed scriptures. This list is not exhaustive.

Shouting was often employed or associated with triumph, victory, ex-citement, awe, singing, mourning, praise and rejoicing. (I Thessalonians 4:16, Acts 12:22, Zechariah 9:9, Zechariah 4:7, Zephaniah 3:14, Amos 2:22, Amos 1:14, Lamentations 3:8, Jeremiah 51:14, Jeremiah 50:15, etc.) Remember the wall of Jericho? The people shouted, based on divine man-date, at the wall of Jericho, not at God.

I can babble a multitude of words at the highest range of my voice and still not hit the mark. Or I can, in my normal voice, speak the word as I pray. Or better still pray in an unknown language when I am short of words. Heaven's authority backs my words and I know fully well also that Jesus makes intercession for us and the Holy Spirit helps us to pray. Remember that when Jesus was being tempted, Satan challenged him and Jesus faced the challenge headlong with the 'word'. He didn't go into a battle of wits or even shouting matches. He spoke with authority. And we have been given the same authority. (Luke 10:19)

Precision and power are crucial.

Then again, there's a time to shout right? Yes. When you wield au-thority against the enemy. You can shout him down. The Spirit of God fuels your shout. You can shout yourself to victory. Like I mentioned ear-lier, you just don't shout to pray, you shout for victory.

When you do shout, is it out of fear- a feeling that you need to be heard, or out of victory- the finished work of Christ? That is the pertinent question.

Ponder this:

Shout to rejoice! Shout for victory! Even when you whisper to God, you come out shouting! You roar like the lion that you are.

7. Adam, Pain and Hackers

God can right
What is wrong.
God can protect
The needy.
God can fill
Every void
We fill with
Life's imperfections
God is more than enough
For you and me

Adam, pain and hackers… What do they have in common? We'll see just now.

I set up a personalized website years ago and within days of uploading a few of my articles, viola, the screen went from white to an ominous black with big bold red letters that read 'your website has been hacked from Syria by people who hate your message'. Never mind the threats, what about the skull and bones? That I didn't like at all. I felt a funny sick feeling as if a total stranger just got a glimpse of my bedroom through my window. Weird creepy feeling! In the meantime, I had a writing itch I needed to scratch.

I don't know why my spanking brand new website was a target of a sicko, but, and I'm shrugging, who cares. And that's that about the hackers. Now for some Adam!

I rarely watch the news, especially CNN. I know I should keep abreast of the world's situation report, but have you noticed how negative the news is? It's always this bombing or that shooting and everything that makes your heart almost jump out of your ribcage. I'd rather read the papers. That way I can censor the graphic pictures. I intensely dislike the gory scenes that play out on TV. You just never know what's coming until it hits you. Then again, I watched TV the other day and I stared slack-jawed at a supposedly gay couple playing happy family with a little boy.

Oh boy was I ever so mad. This so called alternate lifestyle or trans-gender movement or cross gender what-cha-ma-call-it gives me a tummy ache and a toothache and a zit on my forehead. How is that child ever going to grow up well adjusted? I have a trillion and one things to say but will leave that alone for now. It's just so annoying really. Though I'm sympathetic to those caught in this lifestyle, I do not accept it. God's word in my Bible does not and neither do I.

Bottom line is this: it is pure evil under the sun. Sodom and Gomorrah got a slap with fire and brimstone for this same vice and here we are in the 21st century playing diplomacy. As the saying goes, God made Adam and Eve, not Adam and Steve.

I cannot imagine being married to a woman or even hooking up with one. What would we be doing? Don't work up your imagination. Don't even go there. It's pointless and…pointless.

And two minutes later, CNN features on Piers Morgan, a 19-year-old guy who murdered his parents and who is now serving a 40-year jail term. A team of psychologists and psychoanalysts discusses the issue and throws ideas back and forth while the guy attributed his actions to an unstable mental 'perception'.

Forgive me for being so simplistic with everything. It's all good to psychoanalyze, but the truth, the bottom line is that these are signs of the end-times. What would possess a man to kill the parents that gave birth to him? There is obvious spiritual, moral, societal decay perpetrated by Adam yielding the baton to the wrong runner. And so the prince of the world, wielding a stolen baton, saturates the society with ideas and ideologies meant to destroy sanity and innocence. Eden, Adam and Eve infuriated him so he sought out and is still seeking out ways to make nonsense of God's co-creators. He gains a foothold every time he suggests we defy God's word and order. Every time we deviate from God's command we yield to the devil. No middle point there at all.

These lifestyle changers deem that God was not smart enough in creating Eve for Adam. He missed out Steve. Really? We can't preach the truth because it offends their sensibilities. Really? We have to stay mute so everyone can be happy. Really?

The world is in pain, big time. And pain is good. Pain is a sign that something is wrong and needs to be fixed. If you felt no pain or discomfort you'd never visit a doctor and if you were dying of cancer, you'd never know. So pain is good. It lets you get help. The world is in pain and we the believers, although we have the answers, which of course the world will reject, have the mandate to preach the good news to the world. God didn't say solve all the problems in the world. He said to (do) preach and (be) live as the 'salt' and 'light' of the world. The solution to the world's problem is the gospel of Jesus Christ.

Except a man be born again, He cannot see nor enter the kingdom of God.

But the question is, does the world even know it's in pain? Do the hackers of this world know they are in pain? Do the alternate lifestyle people know they're in pain? Do the killers and murderers of this world know they're in pain? The magnitude of the pain of sin is as deep and old as the age of this world. "Is there no balm in Gilead; is there no physician there? Why then is not the health of the daughter of my people recovered?" Jeremiah 8:22

Sin is a sickness. It is like a deep gash or wound festering but the world is numb to its pain. Yet we play out its symptoms in our lives. Jesus is the salve, the ointment, the surgeon, and the healer for the world's pain. Jesus can and will heal, save and deliver as many as will accept Him as Lord and Saviour.

Ponder this:

When you're in pain who do you run to? Who can you ultimately trust to not use your moment of weakness against you? Let me commend my Lord and Saviour Jesus to you. You can trust Him with your pain.

8. This Picture Is Warped

The picture that awakens
The thoughts of men,
Of a formidable foe
Beside our Saviour,
Is nothing short of
Half a story
For my Saviour is mighty,
Mighty indeed!
No creature can stand
And not bow
Before His presence.

Do you know that picture of Jesus and the devil sitting across from each other on a table with their hands clasped together in an arm wrestle? Do you? That picture has the devil looking really grotesque with horns growing out of his head. A fearful picture indeed!

The enemy of our soul has always wanted to play us from the point of disadvantage. And so often the images we have of him are distorted and fearful. It's deliberate. It's to make him look more formidable than he is. Yes, he's a formidable enemy and one we can never take on without the advantage of our new birth, without the name and the blood of Jesus. Now that we have been seated with Christ in heavenly places FAR ABOVE all principalities…our position has been clearly defined.

'And hath raised us up together, and made us sit together in heavenly places in Christ Jesus.' (Ephesians 2:6, KJV)

We have the clear advantage of having an upper hand, a justified edge over him.

Once we understand this, we move beyond distorted pictures to an accurate understanding of who we are in Christ and also, our positional advantage in dealing with the enemy.

So what's wrong with this picture?

I remember growing up in a Christian home where the picture of the devil is stamped in my subconscious: Intensely ugly features, a mouth that snarls with teeth like fangs, dripping blood. There's always some red in there, whether a cape or blood. That could be the picture of any horror movie monster until you add the proverbial horns; then you get the complete picture or should I say, artist's impression of what the devil looks like. I don't know what the devil really looks like and frankly, like Rhett Butler said in *Gone with the Wind,* I don't give a damn.

Still, here's something I find troubling. Why we figured out that the devil is ugly and horned beats me. The picture painted in Ezekiel 28:13-15 is different. A being created beautiful by God...until. That's a story for another day.

So again, what's wrong with this picture?

If we understand now who we are, who then is Christ? The enemy goes as far as distorting our image of himself: he not only presenting himself as formidable and fearful, but on the same level as Christ, like a sparring partner. That's what this picture depicts. To be on the same level with Christ and challenge Christ as though they're equal. Absolutely not! He could challenge Jesus when He was here on earth in the body of a mortal man with the same weaknesses as the rest of us — he went as far as wanting Jesus to bow down to him and yet still lost — but definitely not now. The power has been transferred to us and we are now heaven's representatives. The enemy recognizes the power we carry, even if more often than not, we don't. That's why his best weapon is the power of suggestion.

You only arm-wrestle your mate. You only arm-wrestle an opponent in the same weight category. You CANNOT arm wrestle your Creator, your God. Impossible!

That's what's wrong with this picture. Jesus, the risen glorified Christ and the enemy of our soul are NOT on the same level. Not now and not ever.

'Which he wrought in Christ, when he raised him from the dead, and set him at his own right hand in the heavenly places,

Far above all principality, and power, and might, and dominion, and every name that is named, not only in this world, but also in that which is to come:

And hath put all things under his feet, and gave him to be the hea*d over all things to the church.' (Ephesians 1:20-22, KJV)*

Don't be disappointed, the enemy may not look exactly like the picture you see above. He never seduces us with ugly things. He's had about 6,000 years of experience. He seduces through beauty and pleasures of life. So get rid of this picture. It doesn't depict the reality. God created a beautiful being that led worship in heaven until he rebelled. Get that picture in Ezekiel 28 and you'll understand.

Our safety zone from the wiles and craftiness of the enemy is always IN Christ. Robed in Christ, secured under the blood. Sheer willpower CANNOT deliver you from the enemy. THE WORD, THE BLOOD, THE NAME, are the armour we all need.

I don't like this picture. My Saviour and I are too far above this lie.

We are seated far above…

Ponder this:

Do you have this same picture in your head? That picture that makes the devil at par with Jesus? Trash it! It's a lie from the pit of hell. You are more than a conqueror and seated with/in Christ FAR ABOVE.

9. God Has a Secret

God whispers in our ears,
Words we need to hear,
Of His unfolding plans
And everlasting love.
God whispers in our ears
Words of assurance
That stills our hearts
to rest in His promise.

I have a problem with an obsessive sunny-side mindset. That mindset that tells us that we oughtn't, shouldn't, go through adversity. That mindset that makes suffering a taboo in life's dictionary. We avoid suffering at all cost. I just finished reading about the lady who set a date for her death by euthanasia because she wanted to avoid the excruciating pain of the last days of her disease. I know in most developed countries, there's this seeming freedom of everything, freedom to make decisions and even veto it into law. After reading several comments on the People.com website from people who feel the Christian point of view is bigoted and close minded, I must still add that the death of this woman is a very tragic turn of events.

Making a decision about when to end life, whether others' or ours, is wrong. You can chalk it down to whatever nice new name you want to call it, but it is still systematic suicide. Deciding the day you want to die and handing the reins over to qualified medical practitioners doesn't make it right. I read a comment that said Christians are not only bigoted and close minded but also cold-hearted because we would prefer if she went through the whole hog of watching her life slowly ebb away as she battles mammoth pain and anguish. I'm sorry if most people feel that way about Christians.

There's a law that governs the universe and no matter the advancement in technology, you cannot quench the fire of the sun neither can you stop the earth from spinning. Some things are just not meant to be within our control. There's a boundary God has put around certain things that we cannot go beyond. Nobody has been able to fully explain the issue of pain and adversity other than that it seems God allows it. No matter how much we try to shield our children, they would still experience life and pain every now and then. These are all signs of a fallen world.

Pain is everywhere you look. The Chibok girls kidnapped in my country, Nigeria, have no say in whatever they are facing right now. Rape, torture, hunger, abuse, and even death are beyond their power. They are at the mercy of others. It's sad, but that's the way life is sometimes. We want to lessen the pain and that's very okay. What about when we do everything within our power and yet we can't get our desired result? It's unimaginable to go through the nine months and the pain of birthing a child, pouring all your love into the life of that child and then one day someone snatches the child from your hands. They make life hell for them and don't even spare them the mercy of life. What do you do?

Yet God doesn't expect us to take lives, others' or ours. It's a law God has put into place and the excuse of not wanting any more pain won't wash. I watched my mother go through pain, saw her writhe as the disease ate her body, saw her waste away, emaciated and incapacitated and each day I was torn between praying for her death and praying for her healing. I didn't want the pain prolonged one more day yet I wanted her to live. The psychological effect of watching your loved ones die is excruciating on its own. Yet God would have none take his or her own life, whether you plan it or give someone else the responsibility.

It's a tragic turn of events, dear Mrs Plan-My-Date-Of-Death that you chose to end your own life at a certain date. Good night! I feel for those you left behind. I know you made your choice and now it's too late. My prayer is that the world does not go around playing God and signing things into law that makes life one quick fix. We couldn't will ourselves to be born and we weren't given the right to end our lives either. The secret things belong to God.

Ponder this:

Do you wish you knew God's secret behind certain things? Me too. Perhaps when we get to heaven He may explain? Perhaps not! Life is the only gift we yet have. Can we live and leave the rest to God? He still loves us and the secret things still belong to Him.

10. The Secret Question

The question that boggles
Our minds every day:
The question of why
Our life is lived here.
The questions it seems
Are often of hope
And true meaning
Which is only
Found in Christ.

There's a code to life. I'm pretty sure of it. Life continues to boggle many minds. Life remains a puzzle to many too. Yet we need to crack the code of life to fit the missing puzzle pieces together. When it becomes a whole, life takes on a new meaning. To every child born, life is a series of jumbled code language. There's hieroglyphics in there somewhere. Beyond the basic survival instincts, the jumbled codes come to the fore during the turbulent teenage years. The search for identity begins; the greatest need of any human being. The questions flow out thus: Why life? Why me? What now? Where to? When? How?

What exactly is life all about and why am I in it?

Have you ever wondered about life such that you begin to ask questions you daren't ask? Questions that keep you up at night. Questions that sometimes fuel your angst or put you in panic mode. Let me paint this scenario for you:

A baby's first howl is for comfort and sustenance. No matter what, that baby has a secret question? What's in it for me? What do I get from this howling? Food? Warmth? Love? We all ask the question: This life, what is it all about and what's in it for me?

Let me digress a bit:

What I find delightful in the unhurried atmosphere of the midweek service at church is the time given for worship and how electrifying the atmosphere becomes. I breathe deeply and exhale like a whole chunk of stuff has been lifted off of me. I enjoy that tremendously. There's a reason for worship: to please God. It weaves in with the essence of our being which is to love, serve and worship God.

So I was driving to church for a midweek service, engrossed in one of Pastor Sam Adeyemi's messages on 'Character and the Holy Spirit'. I weaved through traffic, buoyed by his inspiring message. The way he broke down familiar scriptures was simply amazing. That's the power of the Holy Spirit. If you and I walk in the Spirit, as indeed we should, we would understand that there is more tangibility in the spirit realm than in the physical. That's perhaps when we begin to understand a lot of whys of life.

I once read a book that narrated how Jesus visited a woman who recently lost her husband. Jesus sent her to a town, pretty much like Sodom, and instructed her to go save His people. The woman who was a widow of a few hours was stunned that rather than comfort her, Jesus was making demands on her. I paused. I took a deep breath in and exhaled rather loudly. It got me thinking. If Jesus were to visit me, what would I say to Him? Would I ask for long-standing requests or make new demands? Would I lament my woes? This woman needed reassurance and comfort. She needed an answer to why her beloved husband was taken from her. She barely got over the shock of her loss. And the Lord instead asked her to go preach to His people in a lost, crazy town like Sodom.

I think too, that if Jesus were to visit me in the flesh or in a vision, He would ask me about souls. He would instruct me about people who needed to be saved. Yes, He cares if my car breaks down on the highway. He would send an Angel to watch over me. Yes, He cares if we lose a loved one. Yes,

He cares if I don't have two kobo to rub together. He would meet me at each point of my need. But He also cares eternally for souls. That's why the shed blood. That's why the broken flesh. He loves people and He wants them saved. That's why He came. That's why He died.

Though it may seem contradictory, it is a privilege and an honour, when God makes a personal demand on us to reach out to another despite our own pain. There's trust and honour intertwined. Pastor Adeyemi's message came full circle when it spoke again to the core of my being where all that I am resides; purpose and my pursuit of it. Purpose: that was the crux of his message. Purpose is what defines life.

The question of life still hangs in the air doesn't it? The greatest search of man is still the search for identity besides all else. Many cannot answer the basic question of life and the why of it; how then can they help others? Parents are clueless and cannot solve nor even point teenagers to the direction of the answers. Further angst is fuelled by this ignorance. Helplessly we stare at things wishing we knew or have ready answers for our purpose. The pursuit of 'why life' and our purpose in it is still on-going. We hope for some deeper mystery about life and the essence of it all. We want a portfolio of sorts handed down from heaven revealing some mysteries of it all.

Would you be disappointed if I simplified things a little bit? Would it make sense to give you the nuts and bolts of the whys of life? Can we just quickly look at these scriptures to unravel these mysteries?

'Even every one that is called by my name: for I have created him for my glory, I have formed him; yea, I have made him.' (Isaiah 43:7 KJV)

We were created for His glory.

'Thou art worthy, O Lord, to receive glory and honour and power: for thou hast created all things, and for thy pleasure they are and were created.' (Revelation 4:11 KJV)

We were created for God's pleasure. We were created to please God.

'For we are his workmanship, created in Christ Jesus unto good works, which God hath before ordained that we should walk in them.' (Ephesians 2:10 KJV)

'He creates each of us by Christ Jesus to join him in the work he does, the good work he has gotten ready for us to do, work we had better be doing.' (Ephesians 2:10 MSG)

We were created for good works.

'And God said, Let us make man in our image, after our likeness: and let them have dominion over the fish of the sea, and over the fowl of the air, and over the cattle, and over all the earth, and over every creeping thing that creepeth upon the earth.' (Genesis 1:28 KJV)

We were created to be like God, to fully function like God. We were created to have dominion.

Have you got your 'Aha' moment yet? It's simple really. You don't need to read palms or read the stars. The secret question of life is with God, unveiled in His word. Once you connect with God, you will get the specific blueprint for your own part in His kingdom. Suffice it to say, you were created to be like God. How does that sound? Everything else is wrapped up in that phrase. Whatever you desire to be in functionality like God is possible because God desires that we have dominion, we are fruitful, we multiply, we subdue and we replenish. When we miss all these, we start to function less than we were made to, and then we start to question our existence. We function best in God.

Ponder this:

Have you found your place in Him yet or are you still burning with the question, who am I and why am I here? Read Psalm 8:4-6. Okay?

11. Jacob Act 1 Scene 1

Jacob, my beloved,
Give me children
Or I die.
Jacob, my beloved,
Show me the gods
That you serve.
Jacob, my beloved,
How much I erred;
You are just a man.
Jacob, my beloved,
How blessed are you
To have the Almighty
On your side.

I was reading about Jacob some mornings ago and a spectrum of thoughts floated around my mind. In fact Jacob's story is dramatic. It all started with him grabbing on to his brother's heel, then to buying the birth right, taking the blessings. And it didn't stop there.

Drama followed him everywhere. When I got to the part where the women were vying for his love through having children I had to both laugh and cringe. Rachel even traded sex for fertility. You can have him for the night, she more or less said to Leah.

Leah was tender eyed and tender hearted. Rachel was beautiful, but shrewd and headstrong. My concern for her was that she didn't fully recognise nor appreciate Jacob's love for her. She was competitive and was more interested in being better than her sister, Leah, yet she was the preferred wife. Jacob served Laban for 14yrs just to marry Rachel like it was no big deal and it is obvious from the sex swap that he had stopped sleeping with Leah. Yet Rachel was not satisfied.

Add her decision to steal her father's gods and you see a tragedy waiting to happen. She didn't know about, or of Jacob's God? Surely she should have known of God from Jacob's life. She truly was her father's daughter. Which brings me to the main thrust of all this drama.

Consider the verse below:

'And Laban said unto him, I pray thee, if I have found favour in thine eyes, tarry: for I have learned by experience that the Lord hath blessed me for thy sake.' (Genesis 30:27, KJV)

You would have thought that this singular understanding of how God doubled his earnings through his affiliation with Jacob was enough to fully convert Laban. Yet he still clung to his gods who couldn't even bless him.

The God of the universe whom Jacob served appeared to Laban in a dream when he went in pursuit of Jacob. God warned him not to harm Jacob. Doesn't that say something? That you're dealing with the real, the powerful, and the authentic?

Yet he still asked for his stolen gods. At this point I'm rolling my eyes and huffing a 'don't you get it' puff. Come on now. We're talking about God, the creator, author and monarch of the universe and you're talking about gods that can be stolen and tucked away in a little satchel bag or even sat on.

This is the height of the drama in the Jacob, Leah, Rachel, Laban saga.

My pastor admonished us never to take God for granted. And he acknowledged that we all do. I was shaken by that statistic, but it's the truth. We ALL take God for granted every now and then, probably more often than not. All this Jacob drama is putting God in a box. If God doesn't answer our prayer like this or by this time then we should help Him. We therefore take His wisdom and power for granted.

We short-change ourselves when we do that. God's wisdom surpasses our thoughts and ingenious ideas all fused together.

I'm working at deliberately walking away from drama. I neither have the time nor the need for it. We should wait for God's timing in everything we do. It shaves stress off of us and believe me, adds quality years to our lives. You worry less and you live longer.

We don't need gods we can put in our pocket. Those things we rely and depend on more than God are the gods we need to get rid of or push back. They can't save or fill the God-made void in us.

There's often a 'yikes' when we relate 'other gods' to things we put before God. Yet the truth is that we do put a lot of things, including 'authentic' things before God. I'm guilty of that. Importantly, we forget that time is God-given. We can't manufacture it, nor can we halt it in its journey. Why then do we use it as though we can control it?

God first, and then a hierarchy of other things follows. Everything else is subject to time.

Ponder this:

Do you have God at the top, before the start of your daily list? Wise men put God first.

12. A Man Worth Dying For

The day He died
Is the day I lived.
He lost it all
That I may gather.
He was bound
That I may be free.
He fought
That I may win:
A man worth dying for
Is my Saviour
Jesus Christ.

I love watching battle movies, not necessarily for the blood and gore, but more for the strategy and the eventual victory. Beyond this I really for the life of me cannot explain why I love watching war movies, legends, and battles. I can name a slew of them that will shock my fellow women that I could even dare to watch. And would you believe I even love reading about war in the Bible; the Joshua and Israel battles, for example. I don't know why. I still haven't figured it out yet.

I love to watch **King Arthur**, the movie; a demystified take on the tale of **King Arthur and the Knights of the Round Table**. Yes. That's the movie I was watching like a million times over, seeing something different each time I did. This version of King Arthur is not the legendary Sword in the Stone version, but more of the geo-political hostile takeover of lands and towns.

Anyway, this Saxon warlord has been everywhere all over Europe conquering and plundering villages and taking possession. Until Arthur, who had just returned from Roman conquest with his men, decided to defend the land against the Saxon invasion. Here's the critical part of the entire movie: this Saxon warlord had been toing and froing the entire British Isle conquering and winning every war. Aside from the acquisition of land he was getting bored. Victory was no longer sweet. He hadn't met his match both in strategy, and resistance at the war front. The thrill of war and conquest was fading; just another village to conquer, he thought, until he sent a few of his men to conquer a tiny village and they failed because Arthur defended the village.

He became intrigued and wanted to meet this Arthur who resisted and defeated his trained army.

Arthur and his men were called one last time to defend a thriving town against the Saxons who were already encamped around them ready for battle. At the negotiation spot, Arthur met with the Saxon warlord and threatened him, saying that the name of Arthur would be the last word he would utter before he departed the earth.

That challenge whetted the Saxon warlord's appetite. No man had ever dared speak to him face to face with such audacity. He was a conqueror. He had won many battles and conquered many lands. This land he was about to conquer was a piece of cake. He was bored and needed a challenge. He'd heard about Arthur. He'd heard that Arthur was unbeatable. What made a difference now was that Arthur chose to lead this defenceless land. The Saxon warlord sighed deeply, then muttered, 'Finally, a man worth fighting.' His years of training and experience would eventually come in handy. He was thirsty for a real fight. He'd been consumed by the thought of facing Arthur in the battlefield. It wasn't just the conquering of the land that thrilled him; it was fighting a worthy opponent and the ensuing fame that would also come with it.

Do you know that we can be consumed by a passion for things? What about our family, our children? How much we love them to the point of giving our lives for them! Passion drives people. Passion can set the course of history and shape destiny. History has records of gigantic feats and achievements fuelled by passion.

Jesus too is passionate. He was passionate about us enough to die for us because He thought we were worth dying for. He fought hell and death. He fought everything to give us everything. He faced death and hell to give us life.

Now that He's fought all to give us all, He is asking that we fight to gain and maintain all that He died for. He wants us to fight for Him.

Is He worth fighting for? He certainly is.

Life becomes meaningful when there's something to pursue. When our life is fuelled by passion we find satisfaction with each day. We are meant to live life with a purpose. No greater purpose can we have than pursing the man who made life itself. Let me assure you that just like the thrill and pain of battle, there are exploits of faith that make life so worth living.

The world will ridicule your faith, the devil will fight it at every point, but you must be resilient. You must fight for the victory already won. You must fight for your salvation. Jesus is worth fighting for.

Ponder this:

Jesus thought you were worth fighting for and He did fight. He thought you were worth dying for and He did die. So tell me, do you believe He is worth giving it all up for? I certainly do and I hope you do too.

12. I've Got Good News!

His death
Brought good news,
His life
Made news good,
His presence
Reassures us
That everything about
God
Is good,
And the news is good.

I t all began on one of those days when you have that 'when it rains, it pours' experience. Appliance units in my house began to fail one after another. It was exasperating to say the least. As we fixed one, another went belly up. When I thought we had some respite, one of the main appliance units at home chose the perfect time to pack up. I immediately called our repair man who worked tirelessly yet couldn't resolve the issue. Frustrated and running out of options, an aged service man was recommended by a friend. When I say old, I mean that he is old age-wise and also an old hand in repairs.

He didn't look the part. He was a little wrinkled and sluggish, but I was assured he could do the job. Because of the pressing need for this appliance, I decided to bypass the old man and go back to the company that sold the appliance to us. The company maintenance staff checked the appliance and told me I needed a new part. However, because of the Nigerian factor, the company staff in a bid to help me save money suggested I bypass the company and get the part from him directly, never mind the source. It would be a huge discount from what the company would have sold it for. Let's put some figures to this so you get exactly what I'm talking about. Let's do it on tens. So the company would charge say N650 for the faulty part of appliance and this guy was offering to sell the same part to me for N450. Obviously, I would be saving N200. It sounded like a good deal. But I really couldn't afford the part even at the discounted price.

Naturally I went back to my old man. He took his precious time to dig into my appliance and figure out what was wrong. One thing he said though that resonated with me was that the part wasn't damaged. It simply needed to be serviced. Yet I wasn't convinced. I believed the guy from the company was more authentic even though I really didn't have a dime to give him. As a last ditch attempt I decided to stick it out. Nothing changed and in fact things went from bad to worse.

Finance forced me to run back to the old man. Then one day we had a breakthrough. The relief was too great. We didn't need to spend another dime. The part was serviced as he suggested, fixed, and it was as good as new. It was just something to do with the lubricant, which made the hydraulic engine inside to grind to a halt. That was all. It wasn't anything major. On the brink of celebrating our eventual breakthrough, the company man, whom I had not heard from in over a week, called and shouted on the phone, 'I've got good news!' My heart was thumping fast. I was thinking of so many scenarios. Perhaps, I was going to get another part for free or...well, realistically maybe to have it reaffirmed that I didn't need a new part. What was the good news? He got a further discount from another branch and this time around it was going to cost me N250 rather than N450.

Well, I had just spent zero naira, maybe some loose change, to get my appliance fixed and someone else wants to charge me N250 and calls it 'good news'. What ought to be my reaction to this news; elation, or confusion? Neither. I was being sold a lie at a great cost and I was meant to rejoice because it was supposed to be 'good news!'

Whoops! I almost got sold a lie. I would have paid dearly for a lie. That was no 'good news'.

When Jesus paid the price for our freedom, health, and prosperity on the cross, it was a once and for all payment. We didn't need to pay for it again nor did we have to add anything to the finished work. We simply needed to maintain the victory given to us. The devil will come and tell us that we have to pay another price and in fact convince us our life (the part) is damaged and of no use. He hopes to make us forget that someone has already paid for a new life; the kind of life lived in Christ Jesus. Sometimes we fail and fall, but we just need to get a quick repair and get back up. Yet the devil will whisper that we're still not good enough, we need to pay some sort of penance or penalty. That's why some people keep trying to get on God's good side with constant works or some acts of penance.

Just like my appliance part, when things get rusty and hinges creak it means it's time to get oiled again. Get back to the presence of God. There's no more sacrifice that we can make anymore. We simply call on the power of the original sacrifice made and sealed with the blood of Jesus.

'But this man, after He had offered one sacrifice for sins for ever, sat down on the right hand of God; From henceforth expecting till His enemies be made His footstool. For by one offering He hath perfected for ever them that are sanctified.' (Hebrews 10:12-14, KJV)

I've got 'good news' for you. It's that God loves you so much that He sent Jesus to die for you to redeem you from death and destruction. No other news is greater than that.

Ponder this:

Have you heard the 'good news'? John 3:16 gives that assurance. Go read it again and again. Be assured, there's good news. The real and authentic 'good news'.

13. He's Crazy About Me

God thinks the world of
You.
God gave it all up for
You.
God wants the best for
You.
God loves you
Best of all.

As I settled into my seat on board a flight to Louisiana, en-route Houston many years ago, the pilot announced our ten-hour journey. I was disenchanted with the prospect of a long-haul flight; it came as a rude shock as I'd never been to the States prior to that time and wasn't used to long-haul flights. Armed with my in-flight books— ***Plans, Purpose and Pursuits*** by Kenneth Hagin, ***Final Quest*** by Rick Joyner and ***Everyday with Jesus*** by Selwyn Hughes, I set about making the long ride comfortable.

I read ***Plans, Purpose and Pursuits*** and pondered over my life, wondering why I struggled with God and not doing what He had laid in my heart to do, one of which was spending more time in His word. I switched over to ***Final Quest*** and was both challenged and mortified at the way 'I', not 'we Christians' regard titles, positions, power and all of those seemingly important things and leave behind love, true humility, and God's original purpose in calling us. Wow! I could feel beads of sweat gather on my forehead in spite of the cool cabin interior. I was in trouble, wasn't I? Well, I decided then to switch over to the devotional for some comforting words. Selwyn took me on a journey through the book of Hosea and how the children of Israel forsook the Lord and went a-whoring after other gods in their desire to be like other nations. God's persistent love and long-suffering nature redeemed them time and time again. (Hosea 3:1)

It would appear we don't commit the same heinous sins the Israelites committed, but translate their acts into modern day habits, culture and pursuits and we'd see sin issues flying in our faces. In Revelation 2:1-4, after highlighting all their good deeds, the Lord reminded the Ephesian church that they had 'left their first love'. In other words, besides all of their legitimate and dutiful deeds, they missed the point, that of loving God first and whole-heartedly. Besides the obvious 'do nots' of the scriptures, we know those little niggling sins that so easily beset us; those 'wanting to have our way all the time' rather than let Him have His way in our lives. Need I go on? Needless to say, our failings mark us as candidates of His mercy.

At that moment, remorse dug its heels into my conscience and I would have made empty promises to God, telling Him I would spend hours and hours in His word, and the rest of my legalistic plan. I contemplated ways I could make God happy but as I read on, the last scripture Selwyn highlighted tugged at my heart:

'The LORD hath appeared of old unto me, saying, Yea, I have loved thee with an everlasting love: therefore with loving-kindness have I drawn thee.' (Jeremiah 31:3, KJV)

The words felt like hot iron burned into my heart and as I pondered over this scripture, wondering what it had to do with my shortcomings, I heard the Lord speak to me: 'Daughter, I am crazy about you.' I looked about me wondering who spoke, then He repeated Himself: 'Olusola, I am crazy about you. I love you with an everlasting love.' At that moment, it felt like I had died and was standing before the pearly gates. The joy that flooded my being was indescribable. Tears came gushing out and I had to muffle the scream that tore at my throat.

When the Monarch of the universe assures you that He loves you, you cannot help but scream and shout for joy. That self-analytical, guilty feeling I once felt lifted and in its place came gratitude. I was grateful, so grateful that He loves me in spite of me (Deuteronomy 7:7-9). It is His nature to love.

I believe we would spend eternity trying to figure out God's love for us and I'm confident that we would fail miserably. God's love is a covenantal term. God's point is that His love was not a momentary impulse, but an **everlasting** commitment. It simply never ever fails. In Jeremiah 31:3; the word 'Everlasting' from the NIV version translates to "Unfailing love'. The original Hebrew meaning for 'Unfailing love is Hesed'. Hesed conveys more than mere affection, the word encompasses faithfulness and devotion as well. God's love does not change with difficult circumstances or fickle moods; even when we're unfaithful and ungrateful. *'If we are faithless, he remains faithful.' (2 Timothy 2:13, RSV).*

God reaches toward His people with kindness motivated by deep and everlasting love. He is eager to do the best for them if they will only let Him. After many words of warning about sin, this reminder of God's magnificent love is a breath of fresh air. Rather than thinking of God with dread, look carefully and see Him lovingly drawing us toward Himself.

In Malachi 1:2, the Bible says God loved and chose Jacob. It had nothing to do with Jacob's ethics, but everything to do with God's wisdom. He loved David in spite of his many weaknesses and sins too.

To balance this up let me say categorically that God never ever condones sins (1 Peter 1:16). But oh, He loves us and urges us to confess and forsake our sin (1 John 1:9), and choose Him, choose holiness without which no man can see God.

As the pilot announced our arrival, I beamed with delight not just because that leg of our journey had come to an end but also because during that period of quietness and fellowship, the Lord had with me filled me with an assurance of His love for me. He loves me and I will forever be grateful that He chose me from the foundations of the world to show me His love.

If you have not met my Father, the Monarch of the universe, the King of Kings and Lord of Lords, the One from Whose face the heaven and the earth fled, at the blast of Whose nostrils the foundations of the world were uncovered, the I AM THAT I AM, the Omnipotent God; I urge you by the mercies of God to give your heart to Him. You have everything to gain.

On the other hand, if you have known Him, then be assured that God loves you with an everlasting love. Amen!

The LORD hath appeared of old unto me, saying, Yea, I have loved thee with an everlasting love (unfailing love): therefore with loving-kindness have I drawn thee. (Jeremiah 31:3, KJV)

Ponder this:

Do you know God is crazy about you? Don't doubt God's love based on the trials and adversity you go through. God's love is constant. Believe it. Will you?

14. Much More Than Me

It wasn't me
Who took all the pain,
It was me
Who had much to gain.
It wasn't me
Who died on the Cross,
It was me
Who gained much at a cost.
It wasn't all about me
It was more than me.

'Jeeeeesus, help me!' I bawled.

The doctor took one long look at me and resumed her procedure as though oblivious to my pain. The catheter she fed into the vein in my upper arm plunged me into intense agony. It hurt like nothing I had ever experienced before. This was a deep-vein intravenous and not the usual one on the wrist. Short of yelling the place down, I was in super turmoil as she yanked the catheter out again. She poked and prodded, looking for a good vein, and I sang *yee o* with every jolt of pain. Modesty was not required at this time; I just had to give vent to my discomfort.

It took an excruciating thirty minutes of threading needles through my delicate skin before we finally had a breakthrough. Did I breathe a sigh of relief? Not yet. It was just the beginning of the journey and it was too late to back out. Had I known it would hurt this much, I might have delayed the procedure and worked harder at getting divine healing; painlessly. Then again this procedure was needful and had I backed down I would have chosen a life-threatening option.

If the Lord revealed every hurdle, pain or valley we'd pass through before time, many of us might think twice about going on with Him. However, God in His infinite wisdom reveals the glory to come so that it would cushion us against thoughts of hopelessness when we momentarily swing through the valley.

Catheter in place, surgical gown donned and final prayer mumbled, I took the short steps down the hallway to the white room. Lying on the cold hard table, I stared at the ceiling refusing to admire or even acknowledge the little gadgets displayed for butchery. My heart thumped wildly. Scenarios of life bombarded my thoughts, pretty much like 'my life flashing slowly, slowly before my eyes'.

You know the all-important question people often ask when they're in this kind of situation: 'Will I die?'

The question I asked was, 'Lord, did I not reckon myself healed?' I was desperate to know if all my confessions, prayers, study and stance of faith were not enough to qualify me for a miracle, because I saw myself healed.

Here's a quick reminder of how faith works: Faith is energized by a good grasp of God's word, an absolute trust in God that translates to immediate action. Just as the Bible shows:

'If you have faith as a mustard seed, you can say to this mulberry tree, 'Be pulled up by the roots and be planted in the sea,' and it would obey you.' (Luke 17:6, NKJV).

The Lord didn't give me an answer so I went ahead to remind Him of His many promises and why I shouldn't, wasn't ready to cross to the other side.

A couple of hours later, I was back in the recovery room under heavy sedation. When I finally came to, I screamed the place down. The anaesthesia had worn off and my body recoiled at the intense pain. The tender care of the nurses who bathed me every day and the doctors who oversaw my recovery propelled me to appreciate and thank God for good doctors, equipment, nurses, environment and just about everything I could comprehend at the time.

Having surgery didn't negate my faith. God could have used any method at all to heal me. The issue was for me to trust Him. Remember when Jesus mixed saliva with dust to make mud to heal a blind man? We would say that was crude but it worked didn't it? The next day, I got the awkward news that I would have to go back for more surgery; something else was wrong.

Like most people, I had hoped for the boom-type healing where I could later stand on the pulpit and recount how God's power zipped through my body in an instant. However, in reality what I needed was reconstructive surgery. I had faith for the diagnosed symptoms but was unaware of the other life-threatening issues at stake so my faith couldn't have worked without medical intervention. That's why doctors are a blessing. When I finally understood what was really wrong with me, it was easy to ask, speak and apply God's word to the remaining two procedures, which became a walk in the park.

On my second visit to the white room, by which time I had become accustomed to the not so glorious scenery, I had just said a short prayer, not asking for anything, no discussion, just a 'thank You Lord for life' when I heard the Lord speak.

'Daughter, I am taking you through this route in spite of yourself, in spite of your faith. Through this you can appreciate others in pain, encourage and help them trust Me in their situations. This is not about you; it's about Me and My plans for My people.'

'What! This isn't about me? I can't even feel sorry for myself and host a pity party for what I'm going through?' I ruminated. The pain and agony I'd been through and the earth-shattering news that I had a life-threatening issue that required swift surgery isn't about me?

Moments later, the anaesthesia engulfed me in a deep sleep. After the surgery, I was discharged with full instructions on how to care for myself for the next six weeks. The doctor warned that I may never fully recover and there was a likelihood of recurrence in a very short while. Determined to go beyond the doctor's report, although I took laboured steps, I attempted things I was physically incapable of. I let God's word take full control as I spoke and claimed healing and health. Within four weeks I was back on my feet, resumed work, and got a very positive report during the third check-up and up till recent times.

You see, this was not just about faith and divine healing because all along it wasn't about me. There was a bigger picture than my little situation that God was interested in. Not that my pain didn't matter to Him; it did, more than I'll ever understand.

'For we have not an high priest which cannot be touched with the feeling of our infirmities...' (Hebrews 4:15, KJV)

I've had the luxury of instant healings in the past and that could easily put me in a position to judge people who are unable to fully grasp His word for healing or even discourage those who truly need medical intervention. Healing is not always instantaneous, and constructive miracles are not as common. Besides, if we cannot aptly apply the word of God to combat a common cold or headache, we certainly cannot for a tumour or cancer.

But the real issue here is that even if I had enough faith to be healed without medical intervention, God chose to override it. Sometimes we get so complacent with God's blessings we take them for granted. We get out of school with honours, get a sterling job with fabulous pay and trips abroad, get married, pop out two or three kids, our bodies are fit and healthy and everything is just honky-dory.

Now the question is: If God were to ruffle our cute little existence with a series of 'impossibilities', would we still serve Him?

Could a season of lack, for instance, compromise your integrity? Imagine praising God on an empty stomach and no hope of breaking your circumstance-imposed fast. Some of us need a season of lack to appreciate giving. Our triumph over trials ('Knowing this, that the trying of your faith worketh patience.' James 1:3, KJV) could be the only unspoken sermon someone would need to receive Christ and get into God's kingdom. 'You are our epistles written in our hearts, known and read by all men.' (2 Corinthians 3:2, KJV).

But let's hear it from a man whose life is such an epistle:

'And lest I should be exalted above measure through the abundance of the revelations, there was given to me a thorn in the flesh, the messenger of Satan to buffet me, lest I should be exalted above measure.

For this thing I besought the Lord thrice that it might depart from me.

And he said unto me, *My grace is sufficient for thee: for my strength is made perfect in weakness. Most gladly therefore will I rather glory in my infirmities, that the power of Christ may rest upon me.*

Therefore I take pleasure in infirmities, in reproaches, in necessities, in persecutions, in distresses for Christ's sake: for when I am weak, then am I strong.' *(2 Corinthians 12:7-12, KJV).*

Paul's 'thorn in the flesh' had nothing to do with his lack of faith. It had everything to do with God's infinite purpose. If God means business with you, He will ruffle your feathers till He squeezes every ounce of flesh out of you, and remould you to be EVERYTHING He created you to be and steer you in the direction of your destiny.

I then began to understand the reasons behind some, not all, of my adversities and infirmities because 'many are the afflictions of the righteous'. Please don't get me wrong. I'm not saying every sickness, infirmity or adversity comes because God has a higher purpose. God does not get any glory in sicknesses and diseases.

Our lives are not always about us. How dare we live as if we're all that matters? You, me, us, we might be the only opportunity someone may have to meet the Saviour. We might be the one God wants to use to deliver an individual, a family or a nation. It is only what we do for God that counts for eternity.

So my question to you is: 'Are you too busy minding your business, living your life for you, such that you can't be bothered about others? Or can God count on you to be His instrument of salvation? Will you permit Him to use you to show the world what real compassion is when He puts you in the shoes of those in need of compassion? Will you permit Him to show you what giving is really all about when you gaze at the cross and see the ultimate giving in action?

If so, get ready because like a tornado, He's going to rip through your life. Yet, remember that AFTER EVERY CROSS AND THORN THERE'S A CROWN AND THERE'S A GLORY. Sometimes God doesn't put us on display for glitz and glamour here on earth, but in eternity we'll be seated with Him in full view of all.

'And every man that striveth for the mastery is temperate in all things. Now they do it to obtain a corruptible crown; but we an incorruptible.' (1 Corinthians 9:25, KJV).

Now you have a choice, you can choose.

Ponder this:

Do you know that sometimes what we go through is meant to be a motivator for someone else? Our challenges and our triumphs are meant to inspire and help other people. Don't shy away from being used of God. He's counting on you.

15. Glitzed and Glammed Up (Divalicous I)

Beautiful,
Your hands,
Your feet,
Your head,
Your heart,
They all are
Beautiful.

So what are you really like beneath all that kohl pencil and pastel colours splashed across your face?

Really!

Who's beneath the Divalicious looks?

Once upon a time I used to believe I had absolutely no need for make-up. I believed I was beautiful enough without the need for any colour or glitter on my face. In fact, I used to believe make-up was for those who had no self-esteem and had no confidence in their own innate beauty. I was egotistic enough to make it known to all and sundry. Sure, I felt natural and confident. And I made no apologies about it.

Then I entered a phase where it was necessary to revisit my initial stance. What's wrong with a little make-up? Absolutely nothing! So slap dab, I would pile it on. Anyhow, I needed to because of the nature of my profession at the time. It became my identity, make-up that is. From au naturel to boom, baby! As I barrelled through this phase, I lost that simple feeling of being naturally beautiful. Now, I was feeling the glam look growing on me. Natural was too simple. Glam was bold and making a statement.

Then like a tidal wave, the glam phase that rolled in, stripped me bare and rolled away. I was back to Au naturel. What's the point of all this? How I felt inside and how I approached life changed during each phase. Each phase also affected who I hung out with and who I attracted.

During the au naturel phase, my thinking was affected and so was my crowd. I didn't spend time in front of the mirror getting dolled up, so I had to focus on something else. Something else that made me feel complete when leaving the house or relating with people. At that time, my sales pitch wasn't my looks, but my hooks. By that I mean what else I was or had that made me confident to talk with you or expect you to listen to me. I attracted people who saw my inside on the outside right away. Pretentious people faded away with time. It's hard work to work on your inside and be a solid person regardless of externals, but the work on the inside pays in the long run.

During the glam phase, I didn't have time to think beyond the colour combinations that would work with my outfit. I expected to be noticed. I felt offended if I wasn't. My sales pitch was my looks. I became adept at throwing things together and getting a wow response. Sometimes I forgot that beyond the colours of the rainbow on my face, even beyond the cute nose and shapely body, deep inside lay someone who was willing to be known. And I attracted shallow whimsical people, mostly.

I know people who would never leave the room without make-up. I don't mean the house; I mean the bedroom. In fact I know people who sleep with make-up. My question is why? I probably know why, but that reason is not good enough. The truth is you can't make people like you or value you simply because of how you dress up. Beyond the get-up (garb), can they feel the real you inside? Your core that overflows with value, the 'you' God sees and relates with. That's the part of you that will not swing from the extreme of self-importance to self-loathing. It takes a clear image of Christ in us to have a balanced view of ourselves and that's precisely what I'm talking about; balance. The crux of this chapter is: Let people sip you, not gulp you. Let them get to know and value the real you stripped bare of all distractions.

Today, I have my glam moments and my au naturel moments. It's all depends on the occasion. Occasion warrants it. That's all. No reason to glam to be liked, loved or even to make friends. And no sense attending a board meeting looking all drab, like something the cat dragged in. Look the part you play. Dress the way you want to be addressed, but don't let the make-up and dressing decide who you are on the inside.

You are precious, priceless and worth your weight in gold. You've got what it takes, cute or not.

Ponder this:

Be beautiful, woman! Just be beautiful. God made you so.

16. Beautiful On Purpose (Divalicious II)

In my nothingness
I watch His bare hands paint,
Adding, mixing,
Stroking, moulding,
Kneading, crafting,
Tenderly,
Effortlessly,
His essence
His beauty
His love
A
Picture of
Me.

Some years ago, I met a lady who challenged and affected my view of true beauty so deeply that I have never been able to forget her. I was attending a conference up North when we met.

I came down from the cab, rushed in through the gate and burst into the conference hall. I was clearly late by a whole hour. My heart sank at the 'NO VACANCY' sign above the accommodation sign-up desk. I was tired and badly in need of rest after the three-hour ride to the venue. I wasn't in the mood to shack up just anywhere. While I stood wondering what to do next as the first lecture was soon to begin, a lady approached me.

'Have you got a place to stay?' she asked.

I shook my head and pointed to the 'No Vacancy' sign.

'Come on, I can help.' She grabbed my hand and one of my bags while I managed to grab the other before she pulled me along with her. We went out the door to the residential quarters, up a flight of stairs and down a long corridor. We stopped in front of a blue wooden door. 'Just ask of Sis Shade.'(not her real name) She patted me on the shoulder, 'You're in safe hands from here on.' And then she left me standing there.

'Wow!' I thought. All I had to do was knock on the door and ask for a certain Sis Shade and all would be well. Another lady opened the door after I knocked, smiled and led me through the room to the last bed on the right. As far as I could tell, all the beds seemed occupied and I wondered what magic this 'Sis Shade' would perform to get me a comfortable accommodation.

Sis Shade was hunched over a duffel bag on the floor and when she straightened up to face me, I was dumbfounded! I had my expectations you see. For such a seemingly powerful lady, one who could squeeze out a bed from nowhere, I expected her to exude a powerful aura; you know, to look well-put-together, hair perfectly done, made-up, suited up and everything else I concocted in my imagination. The woman who stood before me was a fragile looking Plain Jane who could easily be blown away by the most gentle breeze. And here's the shocker, she had a missing front tooth or maybe an extended gap. Suffice it to say that she wasn't afraid to smile.

'Good afternoon! How was your trip? I'm Shade. Let me have your bag.' Before I had a chance to stop my wayward thoughts from doing more damage to my impressions of her, she took my bags and tucked them under the bed, which I assumed was hers.

'Th…thanks. Is the bed for me?' I asked, not sure yet what the sleeping arrangement was.

'Yes, you can have it. There might be one or two more people needing accommodation, so be ready to share.'

'Wait, what about you?' I protested.

She shrugged, picked up her Bible and a black folder, and faced me, 'The conference is starting in a few minutes. You might want to freshen up so take your time. I'll reserve a space for you.' She smiled again and headed out the door with the rest of the roommates. Sis Shade cut to the chase with a toothy smile and left me wondering what to do next. I felt a punch to my gut. She exuded warmth and simplicity.

There was something about her smile that stayed etched in my memory. It was friendly and completely disarming. This Plain Jane would have left no impression on me had I passed her on the street or seen her at a distance. Except for the gap in her front teeth, I would have forgotten what she looked like.

Sis Shade and I shared a makeshift bed on the floor when two more ladies showed up. She was selfless, gentle yet intense and to the point; caring and deeply interested in people. In the morning she suggested we boycott the congested bathroom and bathe in freezing cold weather outside in a secluded area. When my teeth chattered, she giggled. I failed to see the funny side of the icy cold water slapping my body to numbness yet with goose pimples popping out on her skin she would laugh and say 'Praise God for this weather o.'

Even though many sought after her, she chose to spend time with me. I couldn't understand why. I was content in my own company and really wasn't the type that needed company to survive. Yet I found her presence so refreshing that I would often seek her out too. She had so many godly attributes I am unable to share them all here. Most nights when the rest of us would have been drugged with sleep I would hear her praying for every lady in the room, naming each one after the other, tabling our requests before God.

On the last day of the conference she introduced me to a dashing young man. He exuded an air of confidence and oozed with the anointing. I recognized him as one of the conference facilitators. He was someone you could call a complete package. Tall, dark, handsome with the Holy Ghost anointing. Sis Shade introduced him as her fiancé and I did a double take. I had come to love Sis Shade, the real woman inside, in such a short time, yet I couldn't quite get it. What in the world did this polished man see in precious little Sis Shade? I knew I still donned my judgmental cap and my skewed idea of beauty was shouting in my head. I watched them from afar and it seemed he was all over her while she just carried on, seemingly unaffected by his overzealous attention to her.

Curiosity ate at me. I was burning to know. I needed to find out. So I cornered Sis Shade, found the courage and asked her how they met. Here's a summary of perhaps one of the many touching things she told me in her straight to the point style:

'Sola, I may not be pretty in your eyes or regarded by many to possess physical beauty, but I know without any doubt that I am beautiful. If you ever find anything that glitters on the surface of rocks, it is not gold. But if it is deeply embedded in rocks such that you have to mine it and men would kill for it, then I would tell you it is the real deal. I made an effort to find my true value and the beauty within me by spending time with God and letting Him open my eyes to seeing the real me. The day I realized my worth, I never ever allowed anyone define beauty to me again. The knowledge of my worth and beauty has nothing to do with the way people see or treat me. It has to do with the way I see and treat me. The worst thing you can do to yourself is to hate who God made you to be. Who defined beauty? God or man? I choose to see beauty from God's perspective. I choose to be beautiful on purpose. My beauty is to be an exemplary Christian, to be a perfect image of God and to be a way that leads the way to THE WAY. This is true beauty, to glorify God with my very existence.'

I gasped for breath when she was through. I loved this woman even more than I thought possible. I looked into her and saw true beauty.

While many are hung up on their imperfections, this was one brave woman, steeped in the word of God, who chose to look at herself through God's eyes. No wonder the Apostle Peter said:

'Your beauty should not come from outward adornment, such as elaborate hairstyles and the wearing of gold jewelry or fine clothes. Rather, it should be that of your inner self, the unfading beauty of a gentle and quiet spirit, which is of great worth in God's sight.' (1 Pet 3:3-4, NIV)

The emphasis here is to look inward and not judge only from the outward. I know we often judge people based on how they look and don't take the time to see who's inside. The world celebrates only what they see but God celebrates what He sees. I loved this woman even more and I had more respect for her as we parted ways. I agree with her that true beauty lies deep within; therefore we can choose to be beautiful on purpose. I am a woman whose beauty radiates from inside out of a cracked jar of clay.

Ponder this:

Regardless of your thoughts of yourself, skewed or imagined, do you realize just how beautiful God made you? You truly are a wonder to behold. Celebrate yourself. God took His time crafting you. He rested afterwards because what He created was good.

Wow! You're beautiful.

17. Be Beautiful, Seven Different Ways

Strap on the belt,
Pull up the bra,
Slip on the shoes,
Roll the brolly,
Don the headgear,
Swing the word,
Gist with God,
And stay beautiful.

I t is a known fact that women have a thing for fashion and beauty. The glitz, the glamour, the makeovers and the desire to look good and perhaps younger, become a pursuit of the heart. At the start of the fashion season or year, most feature articles in women's beauty magazines highlight the latest fashion and rules of beauty. Every fashion conscious woman thumbs through the colourful and enticing pages seeking for fresh inspiration on what to wear and how to look. Interestingly, at the end of the fashion season, yesterday's dazzling attires and goods join the 'last season's' shelf. Anticipation builds up for the next season's stuff as people look down on the previous season's fashion gear as so 'last year'. And year after year, season after season, the cycle continues. As a fashion conscious woman, you don't want to be seen in last year's stuff.

Nonetheless, let me share with you another fashion deal that remains the latest ALL the time. These beauty tips will put you over and above any day. With these six rules of beauty you will be complete and perfect, desiring nothing.

Are you ready for a fashion do-over? Let's go!

The Strappy Belt: You know the big bold glittery belt that makes you look smart and stand out from the crowd? It's the belt of truth. This designer label belt makes heads turn in hell. The belt of truth opens your eyes to who you really are in Christ. Truth is the sincerity of the heart. Sincerity leads us to be open to God. It keeps our motives pure. We should always approach God with an open heart and mind. Holding malice and bitterness against our fellow brothers and sisters in the faith puts a big dent in our armour. It also leaves us wide open to demonic attack. Our prayers of faith will be rendered ineffective if we do not wear the belt of truth. Truth is like a watch guard. It keeps us on the straight and narrow (1 Pet 1:16). Truth in our heart makes us sincere and teachable before God. Truth in the mind helps to strengthen our wills to serve the Lord.

'Stand therefore, having your loins girt about with truth...' (Ephesians 6:14, KJV).

Don't you just love this one-of-a-kind designer belt? It's time to get this belt buckled firmly around your waist. *'Stand firm then, with the belt of truth buckled around your waist...' (Ephesians 6:14, NIV).*

The Bra: Forget Gossard, St. Michael or Victoria's Secret. They pale in comparison to this strappy do for the chest region. How would you feel leaving the house without an undergarment for the chest region? Naked right? Even if no one can see it, you know and feel it. If a gale wind were to blow the top clothes off, you would be naked. Guess what? That's where the enemy strikes first. He checks what's inside. Are we looking good on the outside but naked inside? We can fake it to people but the enemy is not fooled. Righteousness gives us the right to stand in God's presence and enables us to submit to God in order to be able to resist the enemy.

'...and having on the breastplate of righteousness;' (Ephesians 6: 14, KJV).

What is righteousness? Righteousness is simply standing right with God.

'Even as David also describeth the blessedness of the man, unto whom God imputeth righteousness without works...' (Romans 4:6, KJV).

Righteousness is acknowledging His Lordship over our lives and striving to live a life that is pleasing to Him. If you're not on God's side and there's no middle point, guess where you'll be? You guessed right. The breastplate of righteousness shields our heart from being messed up by the enemy. Remember that God looks at the heart and so does the devil. In battle, soldiers wear the breastplate to protect their body from spears and darts from the enemies. That's what righteousness does for us. Don't leave home without this breastplate. Your life depends on it. You can't withstand the gale force of evil without it. *'And having on the Breastplate of righteousness.' (Ephesians 6:14b, KJV).*

The Shoes: Stilettos, pumps, flats, anklets and everything else that adorns a woman's feet cannot be compared with the adornment of the feet of those who bear good tidings; the gospel of our Lord Jesus Christ. That's what Romans 10:15 tells us. To reach the unreached and snatch a soul from hell greatly pleases God who loves the world so much that He would let Jesus die on the cross for us. When we walk hand in hand with God and our feet shod with the good news, heaven applauds us as we strut our stuff on the runway with the sin-killer shoes. You can't get them anywhere else. They're custom made, mint from heaven. When we visit people with the gospel of peace we bring not only the peace of God but hope and salvation. *'And your feet shod with the preparation of the gospel of peace.' (Ephesians 6:15, KJV).* We cannot do this without adequate preparation in the word. Without the word we don't have a message and we cannot face any battle. The word is the all-encompassing reason why we are commanded to 'go' and preach the good news. *'Preach the word! Be ready in season [and] out of season. Convince, rebuke, exhort, with all longsuffering and teaching.' (2 Timothy 4:2, NKJV)*

The Brolly: Life is not a dress rehearsal of 'singing in the rain' with a cute little brolly. There's a formidable enemy out there who hates us with a passion. When troubles begin to rain down on us and we're hit on every side, only the powerful umbrella of faith can keep us safe and secure.

'Above all, taking the shield of faith, wherewith ye shall be able to quench all the fiery darts of the wicked.' (Ephesians 6:16, KJV)

This brolly shields us from fear and doubt when we think the roof will cave in. The shield of faith defends our whole body from the fiery darts of the enemy. It protects both our bodies and our gear or armoury. Faith is what enables us to believe and trust in God and His word. Without the shield of faith, the enemy will shoot arrows of fear and doubt and if we're not snug and secure behind this powerful brolly we would believe every lie of the enemy. What is faith? *'Now faith is the substance of things hoped for, the evidence of things not yet seen. For by it the elders obtained a good testimony.' (Hebrews 11:1-2, NKJV)* How do we get faith? *'So then faith cometh by hearing, and hearing by the word of God.' (Romans 10:17, KJV).* How do we increase or exercise our faith? *'Jesus answered and said unto them, Verily I say unto you, If ye have faith, and doubt not, ye shall not only do this which is done to the fig tree, but also if ye shall say unto this mountain, Be thou removed, and be thou cast into the sea; it shall be done.' (Matthew 21:21, KJV).*

The Headgear: In the African setting, during festive occasions, we love our headgear and the more colourful and well-crafted the better. We also love fancy hats, scarves and a lot of times you can tell the ethnic group, culture and occasion by the headgear. Salvation is the starting point in our walk with God and having on the helmet or headgear of salvation already shows that we belong to God. A Christian with the helmet of salvation will be secured with the knowledge that we are covered completely by God. *'And take the helmet of salvation.' (Ephesians 6:17, KJV).*

The Sword: It's simply the sword. The word of God. The declaration of it. The singing of it. The speaking of it. The fighting of battles with it. *'...and the sword of the Spirit, which is the word of God.' (Ephesians 6:17, KJV)*

Gist time: Now we've got everything and we're looking good. We have the belt, the bra, the headgear, the shoes, the brolly, the sword, and you're all clad; now it's time to sit and talk. It's a one on one conference where you talk with the Host, God Himself.

10. *Finally, my brethren, be strong in the Lord, and in the power of his might.*

11. *Put on the whole armour of God that ye may be able to stand against the wiles of the devil.*

12. *For we wrestle not against flesh and blood, but against princi-*

palities, against powers, against the rulers of the darkness of this world, against spiritual wickedness in high places.

13. *Wherefore take unto you the whole armour of God that ye may be able to withstand in the evil day, and having done all, to stand.*

14. *Stand therefore, having your loins girt about with truth, and having on the breastplate of righteousness;*

15. *And your feet shod with the preparation of the gospel of peace;*

16. *Above all, taking the shield of faith, wherewith ye shall be able to quench all the fiery darts of the wicked.*

17. *And take the helmet of salvation, and the sword of the Spirit, which is the word of God:*

18. *Praying always with all prayer and supplication in the Spirit, and watching thereunto with all perseverance and supplication for all saints. (Ephesians 6: 10-18, KJV)*

Ponder this:

We need God's armour all the time to tackle everyday battles because we have a hateful enemy. Wear God's armour. You're better fortified by it. His armour transcends all trends and all seasons.

Wear God's armour and be fortified.

19. God Waiters

Wait
Patiently
On
God
As
He
Waits
Patiently
On
You
To
Wait
Patiently
For
Him.

I stood before the sign and I sighed. Was I now a candidate for this? Yes, unfortunately it had become so. Gone were the days of trim and slim. Things had gone south. I peered down at my mid-section. Yes, again, the tell-tale signs were there. Flab, fat, glob and whatever other unsavoury but true name I might call it. That was my reality. I had gained more weight than was needful. I had tilted the scale and gone the obese way.

That bold red and blue lettering, 'Fitness Club' was scary. I imagined all sorts of machines kicking and slapping me, purging me of all the junk I had downloaded, injected and breathed into my body. Trust me when I imagine stuff, it's scary. On wobbly legs, I let myself in through the creaky gate that added the jarring effect of going into a slaughterhouse. Questions ran through my mind like multiplication tables. What ifs bounced around my mind as well.

'Welcome to Fit,' came a deep voice. My eyes roamed the length and breadth of the testosteronic alien who stood before me with rippling muscles bulging all over. Machines were swinging everywhere with huffs and puffs and grunts from the men and women who filled the hall. I stood and stared until my eyes connected with the mirror on the wall. My fabulous flabby self was a crying shame in contrast to the trim and taut bodies around me.

However, it was a journey I needed to embark on. A lifelong journey, and I was at the daunting start line where things looked as difficult as climbing a mountain without harness, or swimming the Atlantic.

A few days into my new lifestyle, I got to understand what I needed to do to get fit and trim and also to stay healthy. All the chocolates and compulsory desserts had to fly out the window, as well as my couch potato lifestyle. This was a do-over and I couldn't trifle with thoughts of backing out. I had nodded my head at every instruction until it was time to implement it. That was when things went awry.

I had days of such intense cravings for chocolates and sweet things; I thought I was going mad. I wished I hadn't such strict restrictions on my diet. Many times I wanted to call it quits. I compared myself with those who were bigger than me and thought I was better off so why not have a bar of chocolate now and then as long as I didn't overdo it? It was a struggle to keep myself from going over the edge. I really wanted chocolates so badly I was ready to trade anything for it.

Yet that was the beginning of my journey. I still needed to start liking foods that seemed strange to my palate, plus I couldn't couch potato any longer. I had to move and keep moving. I hated that I signed up. I hated that I was obese. I hated that I needed to keep fit and healthy. Why couldn't things just be like the days I could eat a whole mountain and not add an ounce to my weight? I longed for those miraculous days when things were normal. This was not normal; longing for what I shouldn't have. Or was it?

Apparently, all that drama was just the early stages. More was yet to come as the days rolled by, the most important being the need to move. I was lazy. I was averse to any kind of movement. I couldn't run to save my life. I was more the creative/cerebral person and creative juices wouldn't flow if I ran helter-skelter — that was often my excuse for indulging in the couch potato culture. However, I needed my blood to flow unhindered and the stored up fat to dissolve. Importantly, I needed to stay alive and healthy.

What was a girl to do? There was no way out. I plunged in headlong. Straining muscles, flaying limbs and screaming when I couldn't hold back. My daily chant was, 'this mountain shall be removed.' Days and weeks went by and I would stare longingly at the trim people on my team. *When would I be like them?* I would often ask. It felt like it was taking forever to get an ounce off of me.

Some days I would stand in front of the mirror and see no change. Yes, I was told I should give it time, but I was giving it my all and nothing seemed to change. It got to the point where I was barred from looking in the mirror or checking my weight obsessively.

Months into the healthy lifestyle and I had only lost a few ounces. Oh boy, I was so discouraged. It felt like, what was the point of it all? What was the point of the punishments to my body and the deprivation? Something was going to kill someone someday; might as well die happy with a bar of chocolate right? Wrong!

God gave me my body for it to function optimally. The body was created for movement and natural wholesome food. I don't have a right to treat my body shabbily especially since it houses the presence of God. That 'you only live once' mentality isn't going to fly.

Yet there were days when I really wanted to throw in the towel. I was impatient. I needed to see the results of all the hard work and deprivation. It surely must've counted for something. Most days I was in excruciating pain and could hardly get out of bed, yet I would drag myself and go for a workout. Sometimes I would dislocate my knee or even tear a tendon. I would run to the doctors to get fixed then keep on going.

A further few months into my programme after I made the pact not to look in the mirror nor check my weight, I did and it had only shifted another ounce. I didn't know what I was doing wrong; I was following all the rules. I was mad and upset. I was thoroughly discouraged. I caved in and went on a dessert spree. Oh yes, I indulged big time. I had my fill and felt no guilt. I worked hard didn't I? I was busy humming and having a jolly good time when a friend bumped into me and exclaimed loudly: 'Wow, you've shrunk!'

What! Was she kidding me?

'What have you been doing to yourself?'

I smiled sceptically. I wasn't sure what she was getting at.

When she sat down with me she said, 'Whatever you're doing, keep doing because you look so good now.'

Yes, you guessed right. The gourmet ice-cream went sour on my tongue. Something good had been happening all the while and whilst it didn't look like it, weight had been dropping off quietly. I chucked the ice-cream in the bin.

I sought a second opinion and yes, the verdict made me smile. I had shrunk a bit more than I thought. Looking in the mirror every day was deceptive. Whilst I was beating myself on the head, something indeed had changed. I ditched my attempt to cheat and plunged back into the game. Six months later I had changed. I had a lot more energy, I was lighter on my feet, I had shaved off some fat and I was healthier, but it was more of having fun while I got fit. I could now join the challenge team and push myself further. I was more confident and looking back, I was glad I didn't throw in the towel. The change was slow, but the foundation was being built for a stronger and healthier future. Simply because I didn't see it, I failed to believe anything had changed. There was a process and I had set it in motion. I simply needed to wait for the process to come full circle. Something changed from the very first day. My body got an alert for recalibration. My heart pumped more blood. The internal workings had been set in motion.

You may have prayed and trusted God for something. After weeks or months of prayer it would often feel like nothing is happening. Nothing has changed. The problems are still there and in fact getting worse by the minute. The outward circumstances convince you that you just wasted your precious time crying out to God who isn't going to answer. You probably think you and your problems are not a priority to God. You know all those rambles that go on in our minds. The challenge may be an excruciating one. One that keeps you awake at night and your eyes permanently wet. Let me assure you and encourage you that something is happening in the unseen realm. The manifestation may seem to delay, but you already set the ball rolling when you cried out the prayer. No prayer in the will of God ever gets lost or forgotten. They are simply dated and will surely manifest.

Sometimes we want to give up because of the pain we feel and we are so discouraged we can't go on. To feel that way is legitimate. Pain is never palatable. Sometimes we fast, we pray, we confess and live a godly lifestyle yet things just go terribly wrong. Sometimes we question why things are going so wrong. Why?

Can I just crave your indulgence and ask that you trust God in the process? Please do, I beg you. Unless it's a matter of life and death in which case you should be seeking both medical help and spiritual counselling I would ask that you just hold on. I promise it would all be worth the wait. You're already halfway. You just don't know it yet.

Nobody who ever waited on God waited in vain. Check the Bible, it is full of 'God waiters' who got through to victory.

Even if you don't trust the process, trust the processor to complete the process. Had I given up at any stage of my weight loss and fitness journey, I might not be enjoying the benefits I am today. Every single pain I had to endure was worth it. The Bible encourages us, *'You therefore must endure hardship as a good soldier of Jesus Christ.' (2 Timothy 2:3, KJV)*

We are called into the life of soldiers for Christ and we will go through very turbulent times. Days will come when we feel like giving up, indulging a little, compromising here and there and yeah I can confess that I've also had such blah days. Nonetheless we need to pick ourselves up and keep holding on to God. Actually, we don't have a choice. We have to hold on to God. Whatever alternative the devil is offering is a lie from the pit of hell and has death dangling at the end of the stick.

One truth we must understand is that Christianity is a militaristic life. You get born again you are automatically enlisted in the army of God. You have to go through boot camp every now and then.

The more I worked out, the stronger I became every day. I had endurance to accomplish a lot in any given day. Once I walked up a flight of stairs with my sister and I had no idea I was taking giant strides. We got to the top. I was already half way to our destination when I looked back and saw my sister panting and wheezing. Taking those steps didn't even cause me to breathe faster. I was totally fine. Until then, I hadn't realized just how fit and strong I had become.

As a child of God, facing challenges is pretty much like that. You grow and you get stronger, braver, and more skilful in using God's words. Your relationship with God takes on a new dimension. You're never ever the same person after a challenge. You learn to stand against every dart of the enemy and you help others stand too. You become a leader in God's army. Above all, you get to understand that regardless of what you're going through, God loves you infinitely and He cares for you. In heaven you're known as a 'God waiter' like Abraham and many fathers of faith who waited on God.

We must accept that we will have pain in life. People will hurt us, betray us, do us harm and things beyond our control will seize our peace and joy, yet Jesus assures us in John 16:33: 'These things I have spoken to you, that in Me you may have peace. In the world you will have tribulations; but be of good cheer, I have overcome the world.'

When you're hurting and in pain, have a very good, satisfying cry, then dry your tears and wipe the snot. Tell your heart to God and ask Him to fill you with His peace and joy in the midst of your storm. Ask God to hug you real tight and give you the grace to endure. Endure is not a word we want to hear, but we must endure. We have to. Ask God to teach your hands to war and your fingers to fight. (Psalm144:1). Fight with everything you have spiritually. You have access to the blood of Jesus, the word of God, the Communion table, the anointing oil and prayer in the spirit. Use your weapons. Above all, please endure. Hang in there and wait for God. He never ever fails.

One day you're going to look back and thank God you endured. And one day God is going to say 'Well done, thou good and faithful servant.' All the pain will be worth it. Christianity is life, not just a lifestyle. Life lived in Christ is full of peace, joy and power. If anything tilts that balance, cry out to God, but stay firm.

'For our light affliction, which is but for a moment, worketh for us a far more exceeding and eternal weight of glory.' (2 Corinthians 4:17, KJV)

They are afflictions yet they are light compared with the rewards for endurance. Don't miss the reward. Hang in there and endure. The Lord will give you abundance of grace to go through.

Ponder this:

Jesus' blood speaks for you. His angels encamp around you. His anointing destroys every yoke. God loves you. Please just...hang in there. God's got you. ****Hugs****

20. The Whisper of My Morning

I whispered His name,
Though I knew not,
If He would answer.
At that time,
When morning peeked behind
The hands of darkness
And His breath pulled back the fog,
The sun to brighten the sky,
Rolling hills and landscape, He unveiled
The light that streamed in through my window
Like fingers caressing slumber away.
I slipped on my knees
Wondering how to reveal my thoughts,
His presence like balm to a wound,
Like warmth on a frosty night,
Like a Father embracing His child.
And yes, He responded
To my whispers of the morning.

The greatest moment in my life was not the day I discovered who I am but whose I am. It was the day the missing puzzles of my life all fit together. What they revealed was not the shiniest star in the sky to foretell my destiny or the awesome, inspiring achievements that would forever leave history in no doubt about my ingenuity.

No, in fact, there was no earthquake. Not even notable tremors. It was a cool calm day; in fact, I thought no day could be more perfect for ratifying my need to assert once again the non-existence of a Saviour. I didn't need one. I was self-sufficient. I thought Christianity was utter nonsense. I had just finished writing an article for my anti-God club magazine titled, 'Why We Don't Need a Saviour.' I was pretty pleased with myself and was ready to give one final slam-dunk on why Christianity was obsolete and we were our own heroes. My arguments were sound, my sources reliable and my confidence top-notch.

And so the cool day flowed into a warm orangey evening. Armed with my project materials, I strolled the short distance from the classroom to my student flat-lets expecting the day to progress as uneventfully as it had been prior. Two doors away from my room, I happened on a scene that would forever close the door to doubts about my need of a Saviour. Sprawled on the floor was a course mate. She was foaming in the mouth like a rabid dog, writhing like a worm and clawing at any invisible wall, spewing incoherent words. Above her stood six puny ladies who seemed unfazed by her theatrics. At least that's what I thought she was doing.

It would have made for a comedy but for the eyes that rolled right back into her skull. I naturally concluded that she was having a fit, an epileptic episode. However, the obscenities she spewed jarred me because I knew her to be a church girl. She was indeed a church girl, but she belonged to another, as I would soon discover.

'I rebuke you, in the name of Jesus!' A short, stocky, fair-skinned lady commanded. The force of her tone threw me off balance. Indeed, I thought she was puny, but the set of her jaw and the determination in her eyes made me realize she wasn't one to be trifled with. When she spoke, a hush fell over the room and the theatrics on the floor ceased for a moment.

'Gggggrrrrrhhhhhghh!' spat the writhing figure, 'Leeeep me aloooonneee,' she slurred, coughing and spurting out phlegm.

'I said be still in the name of Jesus!' Madam Commandant jutted her chin out and banged her hand with an invisible gavel on an invisible table. Something I supposed fuelled the force of her hand.

'I will not leave her alone,' came the guttural reply from the floor. At that point, I thought, it couldn't be the same church girl I knew. No, something or someone had surely got a hold on her. The body was hers, but the voice belonged to another, a malevolent other.

'Oh yes you will.' Madam Commandant replied. Her next action brought a smile to my face. She rolled up her sleeves and retied her headscarf. We knew her as a Scripture Union (S.U) member so her garb meant she just came back from fellowship. You know, long sleeved clothes, maxi dresses that reached to the floor and multi-coloured scarf to cover everything. The fun of a market place drama settled down in me. I wasn't one to enjoy market place fights, but Madam Commandant's stance whetted my appetite to watch a fight. Strangely though, I didn't think deeply enough who her opponent was. I simply wanted to watch a fight.

'Oya sisters, let's sing, Oh, the Blood of Jesus.' The sisters, five of them dressed alike, began to sing. It wasn't the sonority of their voices that changed the atmosphere of the room. I had heard better singing, but a tingling feeling like an electric current zipped right past me. I had been standing by the doorway initially and suddenly realized I was standing at the back of the room, far from the door. When had I moved so far in? There was no easy escape as Madam Commandant had closed the door in on all of us. Six women who knew this Jesus and four unlucky bystanders like me thirsty for drama. Look where it got me, I thought.

'Father, in the name of Jesus, I plead the blood of Jesus over everyone here present.' She paced up and down, lifting her hands up to heaven. The electric current intensified. I wasn't her opponent, so why was I feeling uncomfortable, hedged in?

'Nooooooo,' the writhing church girl suddenly found her voice, 'Noooo, not that name.' She held up one hand as if to stop the singing, 'Stop singing in that name.'

The women either oblivious to her protest or intentionally increased the tempo of the song.

'I said stop singing in that name,' the spirit in the girl pleaded.

'Please help me,' church girl's tiny soft voice came out in a plea too.

The singing women added clapping to the singing. Madam Commandant whilst still pacing, spoke in a language I'd never heard before. It wasn't Spanish or Italian, and definitely not any African language. It rolled off her tongue like an exotic language. I liked it even if it confused me. By this time, my heart was racing and I had no idea why. I wasn't afraid. I was intrigued by it all. I let my eyes travel round the room. Six simple looking women singing with a fervour and intensity they seemed incapable of physically. Breaking out in momentary exotic language, they moved from song to song and back to the 'Blood of Jesus'. What was it about the song that infuriated church girl? Or dare I say, the malevolent one within?

'If you don't stop singing that song, I will kill her.' The malevolent someone sounded angry as the girl began to hit her head on the floor and rolled about searching for an invisible something, perhaps a knife to slash herself with. She thrashed against the iron legs of the double bunk bed, clawed at her face until blood seeped out.

'Please help me,' came her soft voice.

I cringed.

As one of the singing women bent to assist church girl, Madam Commandant shouted, 'Leave her alone. Don't touch her.'

Suddenly a cackle came from the floor and reverberated around the room, sending a cold chill around. Church girl sat up and turned her head slowly around with eyes steadfast on the singing women. If her head had turned any further, I would have bolted out the door regardless of whether it was locked. The strength to break it down would have come from somewhere. That would have been *The Exorcist* replayed.

A cold cynical smile spread on her face as she looked from one woman to the other. Cold beads of sweat broke out on my forehead. I shrank back and was glad I stood behind one of the sisters, far from view.

'Sisters, don't be distracted, keep singing and praying,' Madam Commandant warned.

The fervour and tempo rose even further as the shrill laughter rose. I felt goose pimples on my skin. What was so funny?

Madam Commandant stopped pacing and directed a stern gaze at church girl. 'I command you in the name of Jesus to shut up and leave her alone.' The laughter died in church girl's eyes. The eyes turned white again, she groaned like someone in deep pain, belched out thick foamy phlegm, then she slumped. My heart skipped a beat. Had she died?

Madam Commandant made a few more pronouncements that caused

Church girl to remain still. I became worried and then puzzled as I looked around at the faces of the singing women. They looked unfazed and broke out in more songs in the same exotic language. Meanwhile, my fellow companions, the ones pretty much like me, caught in between the warriors and the church girl, looked just as confused as I was.

I was torn between leaving and staying. However, something was happening here and I stayed glued to the spot, deeply intrigued. I watched the figure sprawled on the floor for a sign of life. I was playing a statement in my mind; peradventure we might need to give one at the police station. Then I heaved a big sigh when I noticed the rise and fall of her chest.

'I command you and your companions to leave this body right now, in the name that is above every other name, the name of Jesus. Go now to the place of Abyss and never return in the name of Jesus.'

A chorus of Amen!

After many words of prayers church girl's eyes fluttered open. Wow! She's alive after all.

She sat up and stared from one woman to the other, frown lines creasing her forehead. When her eyes rested on me she asked, 'Wh...what am I doing here?' The Million Dollar Question! I shrugged. Shouldn't she be asking the people killing and bringing her back to life?

Madam Commandant and one of the singing ladies helped her get up to sit on one of the beds. They cleaned her up, spoke softly to her, and led her through a prayer of salvation.

Right after Madam Commandant and the singing women told her where and how they found her, church girl began her own story, how it all started. And thus began my own personal introduction to the miraculous Church, the Body of Christ.

For a long time, I had believed in the powerlessness of the church. I grew up in the Anglican Church and never saw anything remotely spiritual or miraculous. These were concepts and ideas gone with the Bible days, or so I believed. Church girl, or Anna as I later discovered was her name, gave a very chilling, yet intriguing story of her grueling encounter with the dark side. Her tale and ordeal captivated me so much that when I got to my room at one o'clock in the morning, I was shocked. I had been in Anna's room since 7pm. Anna grew up in the church, played church, but never really met the Savior. Then she dumped church for a life that held empty promises like mine had been.

Every sight, sound, smell and detail reverberated in my memory. This was an encounter that shook the foundations of all my previous beliefs. God was indeed alive and well. My eyes had been opened to the truth. But I was thirsty for more. I needed to know more about this Saviour I had fought for years not to believe in. I approached Madam Commandant, whom I now know as Maggie, and she graciously led me to the book of John. I didn't have a Bible. I hadn't owned one in years. I borrowed one from Maggie. I threw myself on my bed, checked the table of contents and thumbed through to the book of John, desperate for answers.

In the beginning was the Word, and the Word was with God, and the Word was God.

John 1:1 is where I paused for a long time. I didn't get it. Who was the Word? What was the Word? When was the beginning?

Here's the explanation I got:

The first verse of the book of John is a prologue to the prologue of the beginning of time/things. It started from eternity past, outside of time and space in eternity, to the beginning of creation. The world was 'from' the beginning, but the Word was 'in' the beginning. The Word has a personal distinctness and yet essential oneness with God. The Word Himself who was there at the beginning was the same Saviour I thought didn't exist.

I continued reading up to verse nineteen and then stopped. Something happened. A feeling like a weight shifted off of me. It was 3am in the morning. I needed to stop and grab some shuteye. Not wanting to stop yet needing some sleep and some closure, I slid to my knees and clasped my hands together the only way I knew the prayer pose from Sunday school. I had been defeated. My high and lofty thoughts of saving myself came crashing down. I couldn't grasp today in my hands nor solve its many intricacies; how could I have thought I could save my tomorrow?

I prayed. It sounded like I was talking with someone next to me. I prayed. My whispers of the morning truly must get to heaven. I asked Jesus into my life. I sighed deeply, unable to grasp the feeling of joy and peace that overwhelmed me. Sleep came swiftly. I dreamt of the Saviour reaching down to grab my hand and lifting me up out of a deep dark nothingness. I do need a Saviour after all. I do need Jesus, my Lord and Saviour. Whoever said we don't need a Saviour has not yet met The Saviour.

Ponder this:

You do need the Saviour. Jesus is the answer to the questions you're yet to ask. Life is transient, you must have noticed. Let Jesus in today. You lose nothing and gain everything. Will you?
Forever, Jesus is Lord!

Before You Go

HAVE YOU EVER wondered why the universe and its entire majestic span rotate without tiring? How it all fits together? How the stars and planets respect the boundaries so that they don't collide with one another? Or how gravity sucks us right back to earth, and we're not flung around in space? What about the expanse of the oceans that stays shy of the shorelines? There's a God in heaven who makes all these things fit perfectly.

As enormous and intricately designed as the heavenly bodies are, and compared with a tiny strand of hair on our heads, God cares about you, and He loves you enough to leave all of heaven to come down to earth to die a sinner's death just for you. Life has never made more sense than when one lives it in Christ. Accounts of many people on their death beds often indicate the regrets they have of life are almost always about love and value rather than riches and fame. People often wish they loved more or gave more but don't regret that they didn't amass more wealth.

Are you saved? It's a question we will all have to answer here now or there then. Jesus came to earth to die like a common criminal to redeem you and me that we may have our names written in the Lamb's Book of Life, and be counted as worthy to live and reign with Christ throughout eternity. Life—no matter how long it is—ends someday. But eternity goes on for... well, eternity. That's where you want to be—in the right place— with God. And the only way to God is through our Saviour Jesus Christ. *'For all have sinned and fall short of the glory of God, and all are justified freely by His grace through the redemption that came by Jesus Christ.' (Romans 3:23, 24, NIV).*

Accept Him today and you're assured of eternity. The life of a Christian is not easy. It doesn't mean your troubles end and you float on a cloud all day. Sometimes it gets worse, but most times it's just great. The difference is that you've got God on your side for the remainder of your journey on this side of eternity.

Life with Christ is fun, exciting, challenging, as well as fulfilling and rewarding.

I invite you to please accept Jesus today by saying this prayer:

Lord Jesus, I realize that I'm a sinner. I come to You today to ask that You forgive me of all my sins and cleanse me of all unrighteousness. Come into my heart today and be my Lord and Saviour.

If you said this prayer and meant it from your heart, voila! You're now a born-again child of God. You need to find and join a Bible-believing church in your area. You need to grow by being fed with the Word of God.

Congratulations!

Afterword

This journal is the second and probably last of my Inspirational Journals. I have also written a collection of mini inspirational books, which will follow close on the heels of *Whispers of the Morning*. I was wrapping up my work on this book when the Lord dropped it in my heart to write something completely different from my journals. I have already started work on it and hope to get it ready for publication in the near future. I trust you will follow me as I embark on another journey of hope, trust, faith, and love.

Hangout With Me On Social Media:

My Webspace: http://solamacaulay.com
I Blog @: http://thotsandmoments.com
I Twit Here: @olusolamac
Facebook: https://web.facebook.com/olusolamac
Instagram: http://www.instagram.com/olusolamac/
GooglePlus: https://plus.google.com/117651201998967179616/posts
Pinterest: http://pinterest.com/olusolamac
Email: sola@solamacaulay.com

I would love to hear from you. Perhaps you need encouragement or you just want to say hello. I'm an email away. Thanks so much for reading. God's blessings!

Ugly Is Beautiful

I am beautiful
Because He loves me.
I am beautiful,
Because He thinks of me.
I am beautiful,
Because He made me.
I am beautiful,
Because of His shed blood.

The spiky whip came down with a loud thwack and lodged in, ripping skin and flesh.

My body recoiled in shock. I flinched every time He groaned and gasped, steeling Himself against the blitz of pain. The swollen eyelids, bloodied messy floor and jagged groves on His back got me up on my feet. I paced the floor. Adrenaline coursed through my veins, popping up like caterpillars on my skin.

I could have stopped the pain. All I had to do was to tell the jailors He was innocent yet I uttered not a word. He wasn't looking too good at all. In fact, He looked downright ugly and I turned my face away from Him. I was disgusted and nauseated. He had been reduced to a fleshy messy rag. Gone were the tanned and smooth muscular arms, and the smooth skin and beautiful piercing eyes. Worse still, they were not done with him. This was just the beginning it seemed.

At the time I rose up and gave false witnesses against Him, I had no idea the gravity of what I had done. It was going to be a slow and painful death, a humiliating one for Him who was once royalty.

The hefty men continued their barbaric barrage of torture, turned Him over several time to deliver more deathly blows on un-seared flesh.

Enough! I had had enough! But no, the sentence read: He had to be bruised, battered and broken. Once the flesh is done with then comes the bones. That was the deal. That was the price He chose to pay. That was the cloak of ugliness He picked. He knew what He was up against when I sentenced Him yet He said not a word.

He looked weak and ugly and I looked away from Him.

Then He slumped...

They dragged Him back to the cell and mopped up the puddle of priceless blood. Torrents of taunts and jeers did nothing to make Him defend Himself or declare His innocence. He was paraded before a crowd of cynics, wearing a crown of thorns wedged down into His temple.

Yet through it all, He looked at me with eyes filled with love.

"He hath no form nor comeliness; and when we shall see him, there is no beauty that we should desire him." Isaiah 53:2.

I never imagined this ugly would give me a beautiful life now and in heaven thereafter. I never imagined every scar, every pain and torment, every spiky whip, every bruise, every sickness and disease meant for me, He was ready and willing to take on Himself.

"But he was wounded for my transgressions, he was bruised for my iniquities: the chastisement of our peace was upon Him and with his stripes we are healed." Isaiah 53:5.

He (who?) handed me a damp handkerchief as we stood up. I was too sedated with anguish to notice he was sobbing too. The words 'PASSION OF THE CHRIST' flashed on the large screen, then the words 'THE END' and finally the credits scrolled. If I had no graphic idea just how ugly Jesus became for my salvation, now I see clearly.

For every ugly indentation in His body, it was to save me, give me a beautiful life.

Ugly is truly beautiful, the ugly who saved me.

Ponder This:

There's a reason why Jesus left all the beauty and glory of heaven to suffer a humiliating death. You! Did you know? He cast off His beautiful and clothed you with it. Embrace God's beauty. Embrace the life of grace. He did it all just for you.

ABOUT THE BOOK

God is as close as your next breath. He hears your whispers. This is one of His most beautiful gifts. Whispers of the Morning is a journal filled with captivating stories, moving recollections, and thought-provoking short essays threaded together by the theme of God's grace, showcasing His nearness even in the midst of your storm.

Sola Macaulay stokes your imagination and paints vivid pictures, reassuring the believer of ultimate victory. Whispers of the Morning reminds us that, although we must carry our crosses and endure many woes, adversities, and oppositions, God's love for us is infinite. He provides the strength to endure. All we have to do is whisper, and He hears us.

ABOUT THE AUTHOR

Sola is an inspirational speaker, avid reader, poet, artist, writer and blogger. She loves to read, walk, laugh, pray and worship. She loves to embrace the simple and fun side of life against the odds of life's negative swings.

She loves to help people understand, love and embrace God in simple ways in everyday life. Meeting God in our everyday life and situation is a theme she is passionate about.

She lives in Lagos with her husband, children and dogs.

Printed in Great Britain
by Amazon